Gopal Das Sonkia

100 Lessons to live life Blooming

Translated by:

Ravi S. Varma

PUSTAK MAHAL®

J-3/16 , Daryaganj, New Delhi-110002
☎ 23276539, 23272783, 23272784 • *Fax:* 011-23260518
E-mail: info@pustakmahal.com • *Website:* www.pustakmahal.com

Sales Centre

- 10-B, Netaji Subhash Marg, Daryaganj, New Delhi-110002
  ☎ 23268292, 23268293, 23279900 • *Fax:* 011-23280567
  E-mail: rapidexdelhi@indiatimes.com
- 6686, Khari Baoli, Delhi-110006
  ☎ 23944314, 23911979

Branches

Bengaluru: ☎ 080-22234025 • *Telefax:* 080-22240209
E-mail: pustak@airtelmail.in • pustak@sancharnet.in
Mumbai: ☎ 022-22010941, 022-22053387
E-mail: rapidex@bom5.vsnl.net.in
Patna: ☎ 0612-3294193 • *Telefax:* 0612-2302719
E-mail: rapidexptn@rediffmail.com
Hyderabad: *Telefax:* 040-24737290
E-mail: pustakmahalhyd@yahoo.co.in

ISBN 978-81-223-1280-5

Edition: 2012

Printed at : Param Offsetters, Okhla, Delhi - 110020

Preface

I am not a professional writer; I am a dealer in precious stones and, at that, fully devoted to my avocation. But the grace of God and my Sat Guru, blessings of my parents and association with a lot of people enabled me to contemplate on the human life. My fondness for reading and listening to well-known thinkers generated and nourished in me the idea of leading a purposeful life. We should make a serious study of our goals in life and the ways and means of achieving them. These means are prescribed by our ancient sages, the heralds of our culture, after their varied experiences of a long life. We might attempt to model our lives after them. This idea lies at the back of the present manual.

We have a hereditary business of dealing in precious stones at Jaipur and my six brothers have successfully expanded it here inside the country and abroad under the benign guidance of our mother. We live in a joint family and partake of meals from the same kitchen which amply proves that a business can run honestly and truthfully. We face struggles at every step in life and overcome them with our own ingenuity. Success depends on our learning the art of living. If we analyse the experiences of our life, study the emblems of our culture and take right decisions in a spirit of goodwill, only then we can transform our life into the sublime. This book is a collection of such pieces that will smoothen the path of our life.

The contents reflect the experiences of my own life, they describe how I have been living it and how I meditate on it. I have sincerely attempted to realize in my own life the high moral values, the beacon light of our culture and moulded and disciplined my life. I have made a genuine effort to capture its fragrance in my writing. Hence it records my observations to motivate my readers to live upto those ideals and make their life peaceful and happy.

First of all I reverentially make an obeisance to my parents – Sri Bhagwandas ji and Smt. Gulab Devi Sonkia to whom I owe my physical existence and inspriration to write this book.

I sincerely thank Sarva Sri Nagar Chandra Sharma, Pritam Prasad Sharma, Ajay Kala and Dr. Ratnesh Jain as also the noted author Dr Raghav Prakash for helping me in collecting and editing material for this book. I am grateful to Sri Om Prakash Agrawal (Proprietor Shiv Book House, Jaipur) and Sri Ratnesh Avatar Gupta (Manager, Pustak Mahal, Delhi) for publishing it.

I also feel indebted to the members of my family for helping me directly or indirectly.

I am affectionately obliged to my wife Mrs. Vimala Devi and my son Devesh for the assistance they provided me.

My heartfelt thanks are due to my nephew Sri Alok Sonkia who has read through the English translation and suggested amendments to make the book accessible to a larger public.

In the end, I owe a debt of gratitude to all the saints and seers, thinkers and writers whose works have constantly inspired me and shaped my life.

– Gopal Das Sonkia

Translator's Note

Translating this highly motivational book has been a challenge, which I have attempted to meet by the grace of God. I hope I have done justice to the text and captured its spirit. I have made a conscious effort to make the language accessible to common man and edited inadvertant repetitions. I have added footnotes wherever necessary and supplied English quotations at chapter ends.

I hope the readers will receive it favourably.

– Ravi S. Varma

Contents

Life

What is life? This question is more enigmatic than life itself. Life is not constant breathing. It is not a journey in which we halt at turns of age and then move on. It is the story of man's struggle from inauspicious to auspicious, from darkness to light, from mortality to immortal God. Is life a passage of years like the leaves of a calendar that we turn with our fingers on entering this world? Human life must have a meaning and a purpose. It has meaning if the members of our family, our society and our nation remember us with gratitude and it has been purposeful if we feel self-satisfied with our work. Life is worthwhile when it is spent in the service of others and leaves behind an ideal for emulation.

Life is invaluable. Money might give us everything but it cannot bring back the time that is gone. You may be willing to pay millions of gold coins but you cannot make it take a turn. Life is meant to give and not to take. We must always be ready to sacrifice whatever we have. Altruism is the essence of a disciplined life, for an undisciplined life is a rudderless boat. A man must always be willing to contribute something to others, for the one who dispels the darkness from others' lives, never perishes in this world. One who pursues this principle accumulates merit in the course of life. For him it does not matter how long he lives but only the way in which he lives. Set the aim of life and let it be selfless service and it will ever guide your life. And then life for you will not remain a galling load but become a festivity, not a drudgery but a pleasure, not a bed of thorns but a bed of fragrant roses. If you wish to make your life blossom like a flower, be alert and cautious about your mistakes and as soon as you detect them analyse them but never condone them, never be apathetic to life. An example of our folly is that we decry that our days here are numbered but plan as if they would never come to an end. Life is a festivity, enjoy it heartily. Only those can really enjoy life who join it jubilantly (or they would miss the whole fun of it). Avoid the company of the pessimists, though this world abounds with them, they push us into the bottomless abyss of depression.

If you wish to enjoy every second of your life, cultivate around yourself a small garden filled with fragrant flowers of virtue and nobility and desist from making it a dumping ground of evil tendencies. For this you need an ideal of life embellished with adornments of service, contentment, learning, regard, truth, courage and benevolence.

To ensure happiness in life, follow fine principles of conduct: Be cheerful, Be content, Be calm, Be inspirated, Be affectionate. Live up to them and discipline your life. This discipline will integrate your life lying strewn in the absence of an abiding faith. Life has no use if we do not sing the praises of God. Faith in God absolves us from evils and purifies the life. A poet has rightly said.

Life means : smile like a flower
and dispel sorrow from other lives.
Don't feel jubilant on your success alone
but learn to smile on your defeat as well.

Look at life as a whole. Though we are always advised to look forward, we should pause for a moment and turn back to analyse the past. Those who move circumspectly never feel stressed; the boat of their life glides smoothly on the waves never fearing a storm. The man engaged in a mad race in the world today needs a moment of peace, for we can fully enjoy life when perfect peace reigns around us. Only a peaceful life is tender and sweet smelling like a flower and merits a place at the feet of God. One who is loved by God is never shaken by spasms of pleasure and pain, for he believes that the essence of life is:

Smile while drinking the venom of sorrow,
Emerge unscathed when drowned in misery,
Fill others' life with golden rays of hope
And let the rivers of love and faith flow.

It is not important that we do what we like but we should try to do what others like. Only those will succeed who lead a disciplined life. Unfortunately, people spend more time in planning parties and holidays than in planning their life. We must try to be sensitive, compassionate and unsophisticated for only the tears of obligation, pleasure, sorrow and remorse can fill the garden of life.

What Others Say

1. There are two ways to live your life. One is as though nothing is a miracle. The other is as though everything is a miracle. ***– Albert Einstein***
2. On life's journey faith is nourishment, virtuous deeds are a shelter, wisdom is the light by day and rightmindedness is the protection by night. If a man lives a pure life, nothing can destroy him. ***– Buddha***
3. There is no wealth but life. ***– John Ruskin***
4. Useless life is an early death. ***– Goethe***
5. Learn from yesterday, live for today, hope for tomorrow. ***– Anonymous***
6. Life can only be understood backwards, but it must be lived forwards. ***– Soren A. Kierkegaard***
7. No man enjoys the true taste of life, but he who is ready and willing to quit it. ***– Seneea***

8. One crowded hour of glorious life is worth an age without a name. ***– Walter Scott***

9. Life is one long struggle in the dark. ***– Lucretius***

10. The value of life lies not in the length of days, but in the use we make of them, a man may live long yet live very little. ***– Montaigne***

11. There must be more to life than having everything. ***– Maurice Sendak.***

12. As is a tale, so is life, not how long it is but how good it is, is what matters. ***– Seneca***

13. Life is a long lesson in humility. ***– J. M. Barrie***

14. Life is not dated merely by years, events are sometimes the best calendar. ***– Benjamin Disraeli***

15. Life is not having and getting, but in being and becoming. ***– M. Arnold***

16. A life spent worthily should be measured by deeds and not by years. ***– Sheridan***

17. Youth is a blunder, Manhood a struggle, Old age a regret. ***– Disraeli***

18. Life is an exciting business, and most exciting when it is lived for others. ***– Helen Keller***

19. The unexamined life is not worth living. ***– Socrates***

Egoism/Arrogance

Egoism is mental suicide. An egoist strangulates his own auspicious self. The deadly venom of arrogance tastes sweet while you drink it but poisons your whole consciousness and thinking. If a person ever jumps into this hell fire of arrogance he burns all the noble traits of his character. When you feel that you are more important than others and look down upon them as nonentity it is arrogance. When you take excessive pride in your wealth, in your power or in your beauty you are on the road to arrogance. If you possess nothing worthwhile but still consider yourself all powerful, it means you are arrogant. Among the five evils that taint our character, it is the vilest.

We all know that everything in the world is ephemeral. If nothing remains behind then why do you arrogate it to yourself? Cultivate this attitude and arrogance will evaporate but for this you need humility. But don't forget that sometimes even humility may don the garb of arrogance. Sometimes one behaves with humility just to impress others and win their sympathy. Sacrifice may bring forth arrogance if one thinks that no one before him has made a greater sacrifice. Hindi poet Tulsidas has said, 'It is easy to discard gold and the love of a woman, but to get rid of arrogance is rare'. The heart of even the saints and seers often lies incarcerated in arrogance. Let's not forget that arrogance has myriad forms. If you caste aside arrogance you can easily cross the ocean of this world. This is what our culture believes in.

A conscientious person never falls a victim to arrogance. It is the superciliousness that paves the way to all evils.

If we get rid of haughtiness then even without reading a line from a holy scripture or ever setting our foot in a temple, we can get deliverance wherever we might be sitting. All holy books advise us to relinquish egoism, for self-centredness turns even God's grace into His wrath. Truly, it is self-conceit that converts the deities into demons while courtesy endows your personality with divinity. Pride of sacrifice may be more dangerous than that of wealth Kabir says, 'Keep away from pride, it is fire wrapped in cotton and you cannot long remain impervious to it. Neither be proud nor disdain the poor, the boat of life is drifting on the sea and no one knows what may happen next moment.

These sayings of Kabir are priceless and whoever reflects on them and tries to incorporate them into his character and conduct unravels the mystery of life.

What Others Say

1. An egotist is a man who talks so much about himself that he gives me no time to talk about myself. – ***H.L. Waylane***
2. Pride the general root of all humans. It keeps us into trouble. – ***G.Chaucer***
3. Half of the harm that is done in this world is due to people who want to feel important. – ***T.S. Eliot***
4. Pride is said to be the last vice the goodman gets clear of. – ***Benjamin Franklin***
5. The most violent passions sometimes leave us at rest, but vanity agitates us constantly. – ***Milton***
6. Life without vanity is almost impossible. – ***Tolstoy***
7. Cruelty was the vice of the ancient, vanity is that of the modern world. – ***George Moore***
8. Vanity makes man ridiculous, pride odious and ambition terrible. – ***Sir Richard Steele***
9. Nothing is so credulous as vanity. – ***Shakespeare***

Greed

Greed is the greatest ailment and is said to be the womb of all sins. Greed means a burning desire to grab more and more every moment. You make a sustained effort to get what you don't possess and when you get it you feel a fresh thirst to get something else. Generally, greed stands for a feeling not only to attain a certain thing but to possess it forever. Greed is the biggest impediment in the way of worshipping God. Because of greed we are unable to break out of the snare of this illusory world. Greed for money pushes us on to the path of several unsavoury deeds.

There is a saying that a person under the sway of greed squanders his own life. Man may grow in years but greed never loosens its hold on him, nay it goes on tightening with increasing gains and never knows satiation.

Greed destroys reason, which in turn blows up modesty. When piety is on the wane wealth and happiness also vanish. Greed is never quenched, it simply ends in frustration. It grips and smothers our emotions. A greedy person hoards a lot of things but fails to enjoy any of them. He always burns with the desire for more. The intense desire to obtain the unattainable and the false wish to firmly cling to what has been procured torment his mind. There is no end to greed; there is sufficiency in the world for your need, but not for your greed. Greed clutches at our soul and snaps our relations with people.

People in this world fall in two classes: One that live to fulfil their needs and the other that live to satisfy their desires. Desires have no end and the man wallowing in all comforts and conveniences may still contrive for himself a world of discomfort and unrest. Needs are few but desires are many. We must restrain our desires to the size of our needs so that we and our family may live in peace and happiness. Possession of comforts in excess of our requirements is a kind of social injustice. There is enough for everybody in this world but a greedy person never feels gratified even if seven fold of the world's wealth is showered on him. He still craves for more. To lead a happy, peaceful and moderate life a man needs to fulfil his basic requirements, but if his ambitions are too high he only invites uneasiness. One who cuts his needs to a minimum leads the happiest life in the World.

There is a fine dividing line between a greedy and an ambitious person. One who keeps his mind and soul away from the flames of covetousness can enjoy contentment and contentment makes one truly rich. In fact, a greedy person is like an ox loaded with wealth that he cannot consume for himself. Load the ox with gold or stone, for him it is just a burden. If you don't wish to make your life a burden learn to be content with what you have got, thank God for it; grieve not for what you haven't. Here lies the secret of a truly rich person.

What Others Say

1. Poverty wants much, but avarice everything. – ***Syrus.***
2. He who covets is always poor.
3. Keep high aspirations, moderate expectations and small needs. – ***H. Stein***
4. A man travels the world over in search of what he needs and returns home to find it. – ***George Moor***
5. Ambition should be made of sterner stuff. – ***Shakespeare***
6. Ambition – the glorious fault of angels and gods. – ***A. Pope***

7. Peace begins where ambition ends. *– Edward Young*
8. Where ambition ends happiness begins.
9. ...fling away ambition. By that sin fell the angels. *– Shakespeare*
10. How many things I can do without. *– Socrates*
11. The love of money is the root of all evil. *– Bible*
12. Money's the wise man's religion. *– Euripides*
13. It is difficult for a rich person to be modest, or a modest person rich. *– Epictetus*
14. Honesty is incompatible with amassing a large fortune. *– Gandhi*
15. That man is the richest whose pleasures are the cheapest. *– Thoreau*
16. There is nothing in the world so demoralizing as money. *– Sophocles*

Deceit/Fraud

Deceit may often be used as a tool but its use is never ethically approved. Sooner or later the force of deceit has to give into the power of truth. Call it by any name fraud or duplicity, it always seeks to harm its victim physically, mentally, socially and economically.

We deceive others and are in turn ourselves deceived. The world is a repertory of a wide variety of tricks and deceptions. If we are deceived by others we may seek its redress or claim compensation for it, but when we delude ourselves, it is past redemption. The first important thing, therefore, is that we guard ourselves against self-deceit, know and understand ourselves and as far as possible don't deviate from the path of truth, also we should make conscious efforts never to deceive anyone deliberately or even inadvertently.

It is said that you should never confide your secrets to anyone who betrays others to you, for he might do the same to you. Sometimes to win your confidence the betrayer may act under the cover of love, for it is an innate human weakness that he willingly gets deceived by the one he loves. One who desecrates confidence is a burden on the earth. A thinker intensely invokes mother earth how she bears the burden of these dissemblers who hoodwink even the gentle altruists.

Crooks act hypocritically and evoke public animosity. Wise men shun the double dealers as if they were a gateway to hell. A discerning person should keep his eyes open if he wishes not to be duped. A man must not be so simple and credulous that anyone can con him. Self-conceited persons are all the more vicious, for they preach what they themselves are not willing to learn or practise. They cause more harm to themselves than they do to the world. They forget that deceit is a double-edged sword, if one edge injures others the other is sure to cut and wound them. In the spiritual world deceit is termed illusion or maya. This whole world is a beautiful delusion where everything appears real though just a figment of imagination. Therefore, the individual soul is again and again caught in its snare and deviates from the path of truth.

Deceitfulness is now active in every sphere of life. The worldly relations that we cherish so much are nothing but our daydreams. We dismiss the dreams we see while asleep as unreal, as mere illusion, then why are we misled by our daydreams? Guru Nanak called this world a dream. Perhaps not knowing that the world has snapped relation with reality and presumes falsehood as truth. And this presumption lies at the root of illusion and those who are enamoured of it can't shake it off but continue revelling in it.

At the level of belief, when illusion shrouds faith it changes into superstition. Superstition is a spook that wears the mask of faith and continues beguiling us directing us to infatuation and stupefaction, fraud and effrontery and pain and pleasure. And one day the relations born out of illusion turn treacherous and dupe the man. When the journey of life draws to a close, man struggles to breathe and recalls whatever good or evil he has done and sets out all alone on his journey to the next world. When he bids adieu to this transient world, he realizes the force of illusion, but then it is too late. Yet the soul weeps and whimpers but to no avail.

What Others Say

1. Hateful to me as the gates of Hades is that man who hides one thing in his heart; and speaks another. *– Hamer*

2. Some disguised deceits counterfeit truth so perfectly that not to be taken in by them would be an error of judgement. *– La Rochefoucauld*

3. The easiest person to deceive is one's self.

   The surest way to be deceived is to think one's self more clever than others. *– French Proverb*

4. The easiest thing of all is to deceive one's self for what a man wishes he generally believes to be true. *– Demosthenes*

5. Deceiving someone for his own good is a responsibility that should be shouldered by the gods only. *– Henry S. Haskins.*

6. Open not thine heart to everyone lest he requite thee with a shrewl turn. *– Bible*

Reproach/Slander

Reproach is a negative attitude. Those who nourish this mental attitude develop a point of view which fails to look at the positive side of any idea, thing or person. They always cherish hollowness and bitterness. Uncalled for criticism selfishly or maliciously made by a person is censure. We generally enjoy speaking ill of others or pointing out their faults. A man may or may not suffer from a deficiency, he may or may not be wicked by nature, still there are some who will dig them out and pour the venom out of their mind. It is slandering.

We often speak ill of a person in his absence and never to his face, hence it is called back-biting. We should avoid maligning anyone, for it only begets animosity and bitterness. Those who have a liberal and positive outlook wish to have their critics always around them so that they might point out their weaknesses and help them to overcome them and make their life irreproachable.

Purposeful and positive criticism plays a prominent role in developing our personality. But it does not generally happen, for the critic is not often discriminating and the victim not tolerant. Consequently, anxiety, uneasiness and aversion swell. The habit of reprehending is infectious. The man who speaks ill of others before you, will slander you before them. We must clearly understand that the doors of success are closed for the one who upbraids others or blames them behind their back. There is nothing better than finding out our own faults and dislodging them.

Awakening of interest in self-criticism indicates that you have set out scrutinizing your lodgings. Eschew all forms of disparagement except self-blame. You may be innocent and unsullied like the snow, even then you are not immune to reproof. Don't sling mud at any one. May be you might have missed the mark but you have soiled your own hands. To rise above the desire to traduce others always remember it is a sin to tell a lie, a greater sin to reproach an innocent person while reprehension tops all the sins. Those who admonish others must first cast a glance at their own conduct and behaviour because if your doorsteps are dirty you have no right to rebuke your neighbour for the dirt lying strewn on his roof. The right to revile does not befit those who are submerged in mud up to their neck. They need not criticize little blemishes in others. It is a gospel truth that when you point out a finger at other's faults your other three fingers point to your self.

It is easy to vilify others, for only an idle fellow will indulge in it. One should peep inside himself to see what rubbish lies strewn about there. You are not willing to sweep your courtyard clean but tell others that the road outside their house is littered.

You have sullied the portrait of your character with offensive colours, but shamelessly point out the faults others have in theirs. A man should appreciate the beauty of one's drawing room and not criticize the filthy junkyard. Like a house, life has both a drawing room and a junkyard. A guest is welcomed in a drawing room and he is expected to admire its decor and not to discuss the untidiness of the rest of the house. We must cultivate an aesthetic attitude and appreciate beauty and fragrance that surround us and overlook the heaps of rubbish and litter on the roadside. Restrain your mind, heart and spirit from prying into these unpleasant and stinking rights, otherwise the evils and shortcomings you condemn in others would one day infect your own character.

What Others Say

1. Listen not to a tale-bearer or slanderer, for he tells nothing out of goodwill, but as he discovereth of the secrets of others, so he will of thine in turn. *– Socrates*
2. It is commonly unnecessary to refute slander or calumny, except by perseverance in well doing, they are sparks, which, if you do not fan them will soon go out. *– Anonymous*
3. It is easier to reprehend than to correct. *– Livy*
4. He must be pure who would blame another. *– Danish Proverb*
5. It is folly for an eminent man to think of escaping censure, and a weakness to be affected with it. All the illustrious persons in all the ages have passed through this fiery persecution *– Joseph Addison*
6. The sting of a reproach is the truth of it.
7. Reprove not a scorner, lest he hate thee, rebuke a wiseman, and he will love thee. *– a Proverb*
8. A slander is like a hornet; if you cannot kill it dead the first blow, better not strike at it. *– H.W. Shaw*
9. If slander be a snake, it is a winged one – it flies as well as creeps. *– D.W. Jerrold*
10. Slander slays three persons; the speaker, the spoken to; and the spoken of. *– Hebrew Proverb*
11. Slander-mongers and those who listen to slander, if I had my way, would all be strung up, the talkers by the tongue, the listeners by the ears. *– Plautus*
12. To murder character is as truly a crime as to murder the body; the tongue of the slanderer is brother to the dagger of the assassin. *– Tryon Edwards.*
13. Have patience a while; slanders are not long-lived. Truth is the child of time, ere long she shall appear to vindicate thee. *– Immanuel Kant*
14. The worthiest people are the most injured by slander, as is the best fruit which the birds have been pecking at. *– Jonathan Swift*

Sin

Sin is a curse on human life. Once it ensnares a person, it does not release him for several births. The best way to transform this curse into a blessing is repentance. How can we define sin? An inappropriate action which cannot be justified on individual or social grounds is called a sin. Society has its rules, its beliefs, and to violate them is an act of sin.

If our family, our society or our country condemn and hate an action, it is also called a sin. All acts like stealing, telling a lie, trickery, breach of trust and indulgences in immoral exploits are improper and unapproved. A morally upright social life demands that we should not ourselves commit sin and as far as possible prevent others from doing so. Sin does not do good to anyone. The tendency to sin, pricks and torments your conscience every moment with guilt. What stings you most terribly at the time of death? It is the clandestine sin, for with an act of sin you sow the seeds of affliction.

Sin is not proscribed because it is painful, but because its consequences are afflicting and the sinner has to suffer the agony all alone. You can never escape sin, for someone has said, 'Rest assured, your sin will search you out.' Sin may appear pleasing and agreeable when committed but you have to pay for it in bitter tears and screams of distress. Knots tied with hands require the sweat of your brow to untie them. The religious reformers the world over have warned: If you really fear distress, if it makes you miserable, then commit no sin openly or secretly. Fear sin more than you fear a monster. No one can save a sinner except his accumulated merit. Sin and falsehood are the two sides of the same coin, for falsehood knocks on the door of one who chooses to set out on the path of sin. Sin contrives many forms but falsehood is the handle that fits them all. Stop telling a lie and you will turn away a hundred sins.

Lying is the door through which all the sins enter your life. Lock the door with truth and the thieves and robbers of sin will fail to break into it. Truth and purity of heart are so closely bound together that in the absence of truth you cannot maintain the purity of the shrine of your heart and again this purity finds an expression through truthfulness. Make sustained efforts to strengthen the relationship between truthfulness and good conduct. If a righteous person finds a sinner rolling in wealth and luxury, he should not feel that his truthful action has gone unrewarded. We all know that a person condemned to death is asked his last wish before being taken to a hangman's noose, an attempt is made to fulfil it. Similarly, God fulfils the wishes of the sinners before awarding them the severest punishment.

You will not be let off once your sin has been established in a court of law or in the presence of God. The court of law may condone you once but the court of God will never. Let not your conduct be sullied by sin or no one will be able to save you from hell fire. The punishment for a sin might extend over several births. A wise and prudent person should shun even the shadow of sin to ensure for himself a peaceful life of ease and happiness.

What Others Say

1. Be sure your sin will find you out. – ***Numbers 32:23***
2. The wages of sin is death. – ***Romans 6.23***
3. Pleasure's a sin, and sometimes sin's a pleasure. – ***Lord Byron***
4. All fashionable vices pass for virtues. – ***Moliere***

5. When the passions become masters, they are vices. – *Pascal*
6. For lawless joys a bitter ending waits. – *Pindar*
7. Other man's sins are before our eyes, our own sins are behind our back. – *L.A. Seneca*
8. Sin is an offence against society, as well as God. – *Alfred Wilson*
9. Everyone who commits sin is the slave of sin. – *St. Ambrose*
10. Pride, lust and evil actions are all sins. – *Bible*
11. Sin brings disgrace. – *Proverb*
12. Just as iron rust accumulates and self born, eats itself away, so with the man who sinneth, day by day. His own deeds to destruction lead him on. – *Buddha*
13. Ignorance is not innocence but sin. – *Robert Browning*

Jealousy

Jealousy is compared to fire. It gives heat and burns itself as well as others. This is the nature of fire. The heart of a person consumed by jealousy is like a furnace that keeps on blazing perpetually. The fire of jealousy burns down all the merit one has. Before kindling the fire of jealousy remember it will consume others afterwards but first it will fill your heart and soul with a suffocating bitter smoke and smoulder every pore of your body.

Imagine a man condemned to death is executed by wrapping cotton all over his body and set on fire. What a horrible mode of punishment it would be. Even a thought of it makes you shudder with fright. A jealous person suffers just like that. He burns with envy at the progress of others and the flames of that fire seem to emerge from every part of his body. Someone has rightly said: 'If you wish to burn, burn like a lamp and not smoulder giving off smoke.'

When you feel jealous you are in a strange plight. You feel the pangs of pain with which you are least concerned. If someone progresses and moves ahead, let him climb the summit of prosperity. Try to move into the place he has vacated, be positive and fill the vacancy as best as you can. Negative energy begets jealousy whereas positive energy weaves poems of light.

A poet has beautifully put it :

We don't ask you to make us like this or that,
We only ask you to pour us into your own mould.
And make us as you are.

A person with a tolerant attitude develops a successful, wakeful and positive personality. Jealousy is an enemy of health for it keeps on gnawing constantly into the vitals of its victim. Dark shadows of violence and revenge hover his mental horizon all the time. He feels harried and persecuted whenever someone is greeted with success. But their failure delights him beyond measure and is a source of perpetual enjoyment. Forget not that the one who wishes to see others break and fail, himself has to taste and embrace failure on every front of life. The fire of jealousy keeps him burning all the time. Bound in the coils of a prickly noose, the man torn with jealousy always undergoes mental agony and suffering, fear and fidgetiness. He is never at case with himself.

A jealous person becomes slothful and his energy begins to fritter away for he is always possessed by the idea of his own growth and overlooks or maligns others. Instead of soothing the path of their development he creates obstructions on it. He gradually envelops himself in the darkness of indolence and the light of manly virtues vanishes from his life. And burning in the furnace of jealousy he bids adieu to this barren life leaving behind a trail of infamy and condemnation.

What Others Say

1. Jealousy is always born with love, but does not always die with it. – ***Rochefoucauld***
2. Jealousy is cruel as the grave, the coals are coals of fire. – ***Solomon***
3. There is more self love than love in jealousy. – ***Rochefoucauld***
4. Jealousy is nourished by doubt. – ***French Proverb***
5. A jealous man always finds more than he is looking for. – ***Madeleine de Scudery***

6. There is never jealousy where there is not strong regard.
   – Washington Irving

7. Jealousy is nothing but the foolish child of pride.
   – Beaumarchais

8. There is no greater glory than love, nor any greater punishment than jealousy. ***– Lope De Vega***

9. If there were in the world today any large number of people who desired their own happiness more than they desired the unhappiness of others we could have paradise in a few years. ***– Bertrand Russell***

10. Jealousy is no more than feeling alone against smiling enemies. ***– Elizabeth Bowen***

Miserliness

Poverty is the greatest misfortune and is considered a near synonym of misery, but the pain a miser suffers is a hundred-fold. A poor person is miserable because he possesses nothing but a miser is dismal though living in plenty. It is why miserliness is equated with the grievous affliction.

Generally, a person who does not spend enough to meet his needs and requirements is called a miser. He hoards money at the cost of distress and depression to himself and his family. Miserliness arises in the mind but expresses itself in public behaviour, hence a miser invokes reproach from the society and becomes a butt of scorn.

Wise men say that a miser suffers from a strange mentality. The more he possesses, the more he desires to grab. He brings out his hidden treasure from the earth only when he himself merges with the earth. Those who give something in charity have sweet returns and enjoy life whereas the miser suffers the torments of his gold and silver.

Miserliness is not a situation-born malady but a state of mind. A miser is like a cobra that lies coiled round a heap of gold which he does not use himself, nor lets others enjoy it. He hoards money all through his life but fails to enjoy it and when he grows old and decrepit and sees others squandering his hoarded wealth he feels annoyed. This anxiety and anguish makes his old age vexatious. He breathes in short pants like a corpse and repents his past life when he sees others enjoying themselves. Then he thinks, had he consumed his resources in leading a comfortable life or given something to charity he would have carried public praise, honour and happiness. But this lamentation is for something past recovery. People don't take pity on a miser but ridicule him. There is a story of a miserly couple. One day the husband returned home in the evening with a long face and when his wife asked him if he had lost or was forced to part with something unwillingly, he remorsefully replied that he had neither lost nor parted with anything unwillingly but had seen a benevolent person giving charity which made him feel distressed. Can you suggest any remedy for such a person who feels vexed simply because someone else is doing something benevolent? There is no treatment which can soothe a miser. His ailment is incorrigible even for Hippocratus.

A man may he miserly not only about money but also about knowledge. There are many who don't wish to share their knowledge with others though they very well know that knowledge grows with sharing, with distributing. Some behave in a miserly fashion in personal relations also. They exploit relations and when it comes to them, they play a total stranger. The word 'give' does not exist in their vocabulary. In a way a miser is a burden on the society difficult to be shaken off. Try to keep yourself away from this malady.

What Others Say

1. The miser and the pig are of no use to the family till dead.
2. To beg of the miser is to dig a trench in the sea.

   – ***Turkish Proverb***
3. A mere madness to live a wretch that he may die rich.

   – ***Burton***
4. What we frankly give, forever is our own.
5. Nowadays a miser is one who lives within his income.

Idleness

Idleness is a sort of craziness. It does not only mean doing nothing but also doing unwanted things. An indolent person is self-centered and always thinks of his own self, his own body and never feels even once in a day that he has a spirit too. This pampering of body is the extreme form of insanity. When a person shirks work for which he is fully competent and makes it a habit it is sluggishness.

Sometimes we are so inactive that we let a very good opportunity slip through our fingers. It never returns and a feeling of lifelong remorse lingers. Indolence is a kind of distraction which drives us away from our aim. If we do not want to do anything, it may be laziness but when we indulge in some purposeless activity it is sheer madness. Both these states of mind hinder the development of our personality.

Indolence has been defined in a number of ways. Idleness is the equivalent to death of a living person. It lies at the root of poverty. 'Not today but tomorrow' is a favourite prop of an idle person's speech. It is always better to wear out than rust out. To awake does not mean simply that your eyes are open but it means to rise up, to be alert and set out vigorously for the mark. One who rises up but does not move forward and the one who moves forward but gives in to the first impediment on the road, feels nervous and disheartened is also a lazy fellow. One, who moves towards his aim with firm dedication and rests not until he has attained it, is truly wakeful, smart and vigilant. 'I shall fulfil my promise, or lay down my life for it' is the motto that marks a conscientious person.

Describing indolence, a thinker has said, 'An idler is not only one who does not want to exert himself, but also one who does not work to his full capacity.' If in the light of this remark we cast a glance at the life style today, we find that most of the people do not work to their full capacity, in other words they are not faithful to their duty. If the people employed in different enterprises do not realize their full capacity they not only damage the interest of the country but their own.

If we work below our capacity we dull our enthusiasm and debilitate our vigour. The concept of work as worship impels us to be up and doing, to keep moving on the path of progress. There are only a few who can finish a task in twenty four hours which others take forty-eight hours to perform. If one finishes in one day, the work scheduled for two days it means he has doubled his working capacity whereas the one who stretches one day's work over two days has lost one day of his life. Thus by casting away your indolence and dispelling your lethargy you not only fortify your life force but also develop your assiduity. Indolence gradually makes us lethargic, saps our enthusiasm, lowers our morale and paves the way to our doom.

What Others Say

1. Laziness may appear attractive, but work gives satisfaction. *– Anne Frank*
2. Difficulty is, for the most part, the daughter of idleness. *– Dr. Johnsen*
3. Idleness is the root of all mischief.
4. Laziness travels so slowly that poverty soon overtakes him. *– Benjamin Franklin*
5. There are two cardinal sins from which others spring – impatience and laziness.

6. Absence of occupation is not rest. A mind quite vacant is a mind distressed. – ***William Cowper***

7. It were better to live one single day in the commencement of strong endeavour than to live a hundred years of idleness and lassitude. – ***Gautam Buddha***

8. Laziness grows on people, it begins in cobwebs and ends in iron chains. – ***T.F. Buxton***

9. Laziness has many disguises. Soon 'winter doldrums' will become 'spring fever'. – ***Bern Williams.***

10. Laziness is often mistaken for patience. – ***French Proverb***

Evil

Inclination towards malice and alienation from benevolence indicate an evil tendency. A man's heart can be a temple of God or a haunt of Satan. If it nurses good wishes, it is a temple, but if it is a dumping ground of wickedness it becomes an abode of Satan. If unpalatable remarks that are out of tune with time, atmosphere and situation are hurled to harm others they fall under villainous behaviour. Don't think evil, don't say evil and don't look at evil. The result of evil is always harmful.

Discard evil tendencies from your mind, speech and actions, purify your thoughts and ideas and you will rise above nefariousness. Forget and forgive if someone has maligned you. Repeated recall of a malignant action will turn you into a monster. It is a fact that before expressing itself into action malignity enters your mind. Constant contact with malevolence corrupts your good habits; it is well-known that one evil begets another.

Wickedness draus is to pain and destruction. An envious and malicious person fails to get respect. One who brings others down never rises himself up and one who afflicts others never tastes happiness. If you crave for benevolence, shun evil company. For this follow the simple formula. Never support and approve of a measure you don't like for yourself.

Evil rises in mind so immunize your mind against villainy. Speech reflects your temperament and breeding so let it be a blend of sweet affection, truthfulness and goodness. It is a time-tested fact that evil thoughts corrupt and distort speech; and it is speech that reflects the conduct of your life. If your speech is not refined and its manner inappropriate, all your acts will be imprudent and unfair. "Inattention invites accidents" is not true only for road traffic but equally for the conduct of life. When the vehicle of your life skids from the path of goodness into the trench of evil it means villainy has overpowered your thinking. Evil never travels alone; it is always accompanied by its whole family. For example, lying leads to theft, theft to violence and violence to horrible crimes like terrorism.

No doubt an evil doer wastes his life, but he is never alone; he raises a group of accomplices and tries to harm everyone in society, big or small. Evil action is transitory but the impact of evil habits, evil tendencies and evil conduct is persistent. So everyone must make sustained efforts to keep evils out of their lives.

In the language of psychology a person who enjoys inflicting pain on others is called a sadist. Such wicked persons with their barbarous behaviour, their bitter speech and malignant mentality not only sow troubles for others but also plant thorns in their own life; their sole motive being creation of obstructions in the path of others' progress and for this they are willing to go to any length.

In the long journey of life we come across a number of people some good and some bad. There are some whose company and behaviour does not please us. Their annoying manners seem to agonize us. When there are such people in the world we are sure to run into them and engage in conversation with them. It is unavoidable, but the practical advice is to have limited relations with them and if possible avoid them altogether. Both amicability and animosity with the wicked are harmful. Their company paves the path of our decline and destruction and corrupts our manners and morals. These depraved persons contaminate their surroundings so much so that even our Herculean efforts to protect ourselves fail to bear fruit.

In public dealings also the company of the wicked invites only disgrace and dishonour. A gentleman may be straightforward and discreet in his behaviour with the scandalous, may keep his character unsullied but the public opinion will caste aspersion on him, make some allegation or the other against him. Even if a person drinks milk while sitting in a pub, people will take him to be a tippler. Similarly, if a kind and courteous person moves about in the company of vile and immoral persons he is classed with them, for 'a man is known by the company he keeps' is an old and established saying.

Our social norms expect us to keep the villains at an arm's length and draw closer to courteous and cultivated persons. The life of a gentleman is like a fragrant flower which disseminates fragrance of affection without one's asking. It is a lamp that gives the light of love. He has such a vast reserve of feelings and experiences that under its cool and refreshing shadow even the most virulent villains give up their evil tendencies and turn docile and humane. On the other hand, the life of a malevolent villain is like a thorn that pricks and wounds any one that passes its way. A thorn does not change its nature even in the company of roses; similarly, an evil-minded person finds faults with most righteous and kind-hearted persons. He speaks ill of even beauty and fragrance. About his cynical and acrimonious attitude a poet has remarked.

Surrounded by many a bloom,
Thorns don't give up their gloom.

The noble always fear this disposition of the villains. It is why in the opening lines of *Ram Charit Manas*, Tulsidas salutes the villains. It is better to keep away from such people. If they draw closer they can vitiate your feelings, your demeanour and even your temperament. Maintain a respectable distance from them.

What Others Say

1. Non-cooperation with evil is as much a duty as is cooperation with good. – ***Mahatma Gandhi***
2. Men loved darkness rather than light because their deeds were evil. – ***Bible***
3. Wickedness is always easier than virtue for it takes the short cut to everything. – ***S. Johnsen***
4. He who accepts evil without protesting against it is really cooperating with it. – ***Martin Luther King Jr.***
5. No man is justified in doing evil on the ground of expediency. – ***Theodore Roosevelt***
6. The evil that men do lives after them. – ***Shakespeare***
7. Evil often triumphs but never conquers. – ***Joseph Rouse***
8. Evil unchecked grows, evil tolerated poisons the whole system. – ***Jawaharlal Nehru***
9. Evil allures but good endures. – ***Tolstoy***
10. Work keeps us from three evils, boredom, vice and need. – ***Voltaire***

Error

In our day-to-day conduct of life we often err from the right course but when it forms a part of our habit it leads to mistakes which in their turn drag us to the dark world of crime. It is, therefore, necessary to check our mistakes ere they transform into a crime.

Unwittingly in our life we make a remark or do something which others don't like. It is the sort of behaviour that is called an error or a mistake. There is no one in the world who has not made a mistake. We often make them, but our nobility lies in gracefully acknowledging our mistakes and making amends for them. We must be vigilant enough not to commit the same mistake again. It is not a shame to accept a slip of behaviour but not to accept a mistake as mistake is a blunder.

If one discovers that he has made a mistake, but makes no effort to redress it, he is committing one more mistake. Conscientious people learn from the mistakes of others. Anyone can make a mistake but only a fool defends and justifies it obstinately. One who does not attempt anything makes no mistakes, although he does not realize that inactivity is itself a big mistake. The house where a member admits having made a mistake and others are willing to forgive him is a paradise. A man learns from his mistakes, but it does not mean that he should go on making mistakes all his life and keep saying he is learning. Those who hold their mistakes close to their heart forget that these will ruin their life. Mistakes take a moment to commit but the stigma they leave persists over the generations. A poet says:

A moment's lapse, history tells
Vexes us for centuries.

We are forgetful about our mistakes but vigilant for those of others. A wise man says, 'When I wish to find faults I make a beginning with myself and fail to move onward.' One who is careful about his mistakes can make his life fragrant like flowers. Have you heard about a man who accused the sun for not lighting his cigarette. We often make the mistake of holding others responsible for our mistakes. The ageold saying is:

'If man gains, he praises his effort but if he loses he blames the fate or God and with this habit displeases God. If the man attributes success to himself and assigns the failure to God, how can he hope to realize Him? Even if God himself appears before him he will not care to look into His eyes.

The psychology of man today defies understanding but spiritualism holds the key to this knotty problem. It tells that man makes a basic mistake of considering himself the doer. This generates arrogance which in turn confirms this attitude and leads him to exploitation, violence and terrorism. If man considers himself a tool in the hand of the Almighty and discharges his duty to the best of his ability, he would never deviate from the path of virtue and make no mistake.

What Others Say

1. Justifying a fault doubles it. – ***French Proverb***
2. He is always right who suspects that he makes mistakes. – ***Anonymous***
3. It is the true nature of mankind to learn from mistakes, not from example. – ***Fred Hoyle***
4. A life spent in making mistakes is not only more honourable but more useful than a life spent doing nothing. – ***George Bernard Shaw***

5. To make no mistake is not in the power of man, but from their errors and mistakes the wise and good learn wisdom for future. *– Plutarch*
6. Any man may make a mistake but none but a fool will continue in it. *– Cicero*
7. Mistakes are the usual bridge between inexperience and wisdom. *– Phyllis Theroux*
8. Admit your errors before someone else exaggerates them. *– Andrew V. Mason*
9. It is only an error in judgement to make a mistake, but it shows infirmity of character to adhere to it when discovered. *– C.N. Bovee*
10. The worst part is not in making a mistake but in trying to justify it. It is only a warning of our mindlessness or our ignorance. *– Santiago Ramon Y. Cajal*

Weakling

'A strong and powerful person is above reproach,' says Tulsidas, but our culture does not fully endorse it, for it holds that the Lord always supports the weak. God provides him protection without his asking. The question now arises who is weak? Physical weakness is innate or may be caused by disease. In reality weak is one who has either lost faith in himself or is irresolute. Physical weakness is harmful but more so is mental infirmity, although either can't be appreciated in any way. A healthy mind lives in a healthy body, hence both body and mind should be strong. Success knocks on the door of one who is strong both physically and mentally.

Infact, bodily weakness is often caused by mental infirmity. A feeble-minded person is a slave to his senses and habits that gratify senses. In our day-to-day conversation we often say it is our weakness, or it is the weakness of a particular person meaning thereby that their mind is slave of certain habits. One who is strong is the master, but one who is weak is a slave. Our culture does not honour one who has vanquished the world, but the one who has conquered one's self; the one who has overpowered his weaknesses, one who has determination enough to hold his mind in submission.

Our habits make for our mental weakness. Some of our bad habits clutch us so tightly that we can't get rid of them easily. We have so little control over our mind that we yield to our habits every moment. Tell anyone, 'This habit of yours is not, appreciable, please change it, and he will promptly splutter. 'Ask me to change any other thing and I will, but not a habit'. In fact, a man cannot change anything; he cannot change his destiny, nor the speed of the age running fast, nor the weather, nor the moon, the stars and the scenes of nature, but only himself. He can modify his habits but invents a hundred excuses not to do so.

One who submits to the force of his habits is really a weakling. Man claims to change the world but is not willing to change himself. 'Control yourself before you exercise control over others', must be the guiding principle of a man's life if he wants to be a winner otherwise his moving about in space or scaling Mount Everest a hundred times is all in vain. One who has lost faith in himself loses everything in the world and the one who conquers himself conquers all.

In our country the saints and seers, teachers and preachers have always insisted on controlling our manners and behaviour, our mental states and thoughts, our sense perceptions and passions. We should subdue our senses, be the master and exercise control over them but unfortunately we are slaves to them.

The English word WATCH provides us a complete guide to our conduct. It means 'be alert', 'pay attention to' 'observe carefully' etc. We can interpret it as follows:

W **stands for** **Watch**, stay awake, look at what is happening all around you.

A **stands for** Watch your **Actions**, let no evil enter them.

T **stands for** Watch your **Thoughts**, your **Tongue**; let no evil thought ever cross your mind, let no evil words come out of your mouth. watch your language, be gentle and sweet in your speech.

C **stands for** Watch your **Characte**r, your day-to-day conduct.

H **stands for** Watch your **Habits**, if you contract evil habits you weaken the foundation of your life, and when the foundation begins to give in, the fine structure above takes no time in crumbling down. Strengthen the foundation of your character, and then you will strengthen your life in a true sense; the weakness inside us will then turn into innocence and purity.

What Others Say

1. We that are strong ought to bear the infirmities of the weak. – ***New Testament***
2. The concessions of the weak are the concessions of fear. – ***Edmund Burke***
3. Resolve to be tolerant with the weak and the wrong. – ***Bob Goddard***
4. We all have weaknesses and should learn to make a reasonable discount for those of others. – ***William Allen White***
5. A country is considered civilized if its laws hinder a weak man from becoming too weak or a powerful one too powerful. – ***Primo Levi***
6. All the world knows that the weak overcomes the strong and the soft overcomes the hard. But none can practice it. – ***Lao Tzu***

Emotions

Feeling

Feelings are ripples in the ocean of mind. The surface of the sea is constantly ruffled by ripples and waves. Similarly, hundreds of thought waves cross our mind in the twinkling of an eye. These thoughts and feelings shape our personality. If they are good they incline us to be kind and virtuous, but if they are evil they drag us on the path of decline and destruction. In other words feelings lie at the bottom of both virtue and vice, construction and destruction. We can define them as internal inspiration or mental attitude. It is the feelings that determine our attitude towards an action, a person, a thought, or idea or even God.

Feelings leave their impact on all over activities. In fact they determine our success and achievement in any enterprise. Our generous and righteous attitude ensures our success in our attempts.

Even God is moved by the sincerity of our feelings, for God does not love ostentation or pretension, but simplicity and piety. He accepts even a flower if offered with pious submissiveness but not the luxuries and delicacies presented ostensibly. This virtuous feeling enjoys a special place in our personal conduct as well as our family and social relations and devotion to God.

Untainted, pure and pious feelings ensure the nobility and success of an action. A thinker says and a poet confirms that God appears before us in the form we have been mentally reflecting upon Him. Drive away your bestial feelings; let noble feelings flow in their place and you will elevate yourself to excellence.

Our feelings depend on the intensity of our physical and mental sensations. A wise man wonders "What is an eye if it never brims with tears of compassion or a face that never brightens with a smile of joy?" If you feel joy, smile and if you are carried away by affliction, shed tears, it will give vent to your feelings and relieve you. Disseminate beneficial feelings and repress the harmful ones; feelings yield joy when shared with others but wither out if confined to yourself. It is the wealth that multiplies with sharing and distribution, hence those desiring emotional satisfaction should shower compassion on the afflicted and needy.

Those whose feelings are vitiated by selfishness and crookedness can only be forgiven. Sinister feelings lead to wrong decisions and misapprehensions. If your feelings are not righteous your judgements will he malicious. Lord Krishna tells Arjuna in the Gita that anything, be it sacrifice, charity or penance performed without faith is transitory and meaningless both here and hereafter.

You must always be watchful to keep the universe of your feelings unsullied and untarnished. Feelings are closely related with behaviour. If your feelings are translated into overt behaviour, you will never feel an emptiness or uselessness. There is an innate connection between feelings and actions. Man's ascent or descent is determined at the level of feelings. You can never lead a pious life without first refining your feelings. Whatever display of piety a man may make, he can circumambulate a temple, a mosque, a church or Gurudwara but his behaviour will not be benevolent unless he has consecrated his thoughts and feelings. The mere display does not reveal your religiosity; it is nothing more than an ostentatious semblance.

For the purification of our feelings we should be alert and vigilant about our thoughts. No thief or burglar dare enter a house if the guard is wakeful. Similarly, circumspection safeguards our thought process from contamination. If we introspect our feelings and attempt their analysis we can discriminate between the beneficial and the baneful ones. Gradually the evil thoughts will vanish into the thin air. A scrutiny of our feelings will make us not only conscientious about good or evil, but also bring about a multidimensional change in our positive thinking and creative energy. To clean the mould of thinking we must make efforts for purifying feelings. If our day-to-day activities are clean and transparent our feelings will automatically be chaste and undefiled. Piety and chastity of feelings will find manifestation in clean and healthy character and conduct.

What Others Say

1. Manners are a sensitive awareness of feelings of others. If you have that awareness, you have good manners.

   – Emily Port

2. Art is the objectification of feeling. *– Susanne Langer*

Joy

Joy is the fragrance emanating from the bloom of heart. It is a divine gift that expresses itself in a smile. A wise man holds that the difference between a man and an animal lies in the way they both express their joy. Man expresses his joy by smiling but an animal cannot do so while other life sustaining activities of both man and animal are similar. If you find an animal smiling you can presume that he is acquiring human attributes, and if a man forgets how to smile, it means that he has adopted animal traits. A poet says:

To please you, I've forgotten all pain
To please you, I've accepted all.
My abode brightens when you enter
Your presence adds to its merry glow.

There are several paths that lead to the gateway of joy, but no one can prescribe a standard measure of joy for all. When a doctor emerges out of an operation theatre after performing a successful operation, he is wreathed in smiles. A mother feels joy when she has bathed her child. Small children in villages enjoy making and breaking clay toys. Wise men advise us not to waste all our life in only making preparations but to enjoy every moment of it. Joy is valuable for life but how one seeks it is equally significant.

There are six sources of pleasure in this world. They are : our material possessions; our abiding good health, an amiable and soft spoken life partner, an obedient son and a remunerative education. These make our life cheerful and worth living. The best way of ensuring our happiness is to keep ourselves free from unattainable ambitions. No one can fulfil all his desires in the world. Even Alexander could not do so, hence servility to desires is the source of enormous pain and suffering.

A man who has curtailed his needs is happy whereas the one who is wandering about in the blind maze of desires and aspirations never sees the light of joyous contentment. Another condition of happiness is: Share your joy with others. It is a time-tested and experienced fact that happiness increases and pain decreases when shared. Let us extend the thrill of joy to fortify the feeling of coexistence in society, to see smile in every eye and to make every tear glow with hope.

What Others Say

1. To get the full value from joy you must have somebody to divide it with. – ***Mark Twain***
2. A joy that is shared is a joy made double. One can endure sorrow alone but it takes two to be glad. – ***Elbert Hubbard***
3. That man is the richest whose pleasures are the cheapest. – ***Henry David Thoreau***
4. Pleasure is the only thing to live for. Nothing ages like happiness. – ***Oscar Wilde***
5. Sweet is pleasure after pain. – ***Dryden***
6. Joy is in the battle. The result comes by the grace of God. – ***Mahatma Gandhi***
7. The only true happiness comes from squandering our selves for a purpose. – ***William Cowper***
8. Even if we can't be happy, we must always be cheerful. – ***Irving Kristol***
9. Only those are really happy who have sought and found to serve. – ***Albert Schweitzer***
10. There is only one way to happiness and that is to cease to worrying about things which are beyond the power of our will. – ***Epictetus***

Kama (Lust)

Kama (lust) stands for desire or passion. Natural attraction that human beings feel towards the opposite sex is called sexual desire. Passion is not a synonym of sex or lust. It is one of the four aims (or objectives) of life. Every normal human being has a natural desire for sex. It is an instinct that cannot be eliminated but only sublimated. If one is overpowered by sex he slides towards his ruin, but if one sublimates it he scales great heights. Our culture prescribes procreation as one of our essential duties in the world. If a married couple indulges in sex for producing offspring it is not unrighteous or immoral.

Sex is morally acceptable because it is essential for fulfilling our worldly duties but when it is out of bonds, illicit or lustful, it is an aberration. Discipline and modesty in consumption and behaviour add to the charm of life whereas immoral and unrestrained behaviour is not only reprehensible but also ruinous to life. We must work for the sublimation of sex and sexual satisfaction must be sought strictly within the prescribed bonds of morality. When sex infringes the approved limits it leads to dissolution and depravity but regulated sex gives us elegance and refinement. Among the sixteen Hindu sacraments it is the one performed to favour conception. In the Kamayani, Jayshanker Prasad says:

Benevolent lust adorns the world
That originates from it,
Neglect and suppress it not
Or you'll make life fruitless.

When lust leads you astray, enjoyment becomes licentious – the most pernicious disease in the world. Restraint gives the greatest joy, for the holy scriptures say, 'The frenzy of passion is transient, but its repentance persistent'. Reason surrenders to passion and abets it. It is a psychological truth that even the action we are unable to perform flares up an opposite reaction. The body may he shrivelled, the face wrinkled and hair turned grey, yet the passion continues raging and brewing because the man nurses lust in his mind. Lust is a physical action but by instilling it into our mind we become neurotic.

Instead of quenching the thirst for it enjoyment of pleasure excites it a hundred-fold. The sallies of youth sow the seeds of passion the crop of which we have to reap in old age under the whip-hand of torment. Thinking about pleasures braces our attachment with them. It is our bounden duty to make sustained efforts for the sublimation of the sex-instinct. If a gentle householder leading a comfortable and joyful life still makes constant efforts to rise above them, he makes his life auspicious and benevolent. In him the love of lord supersedes love for pleasure.

For the sublimation of our base instincts we must cast off all sinful and degrading acts. Scriptures sanction sensual gratification but condemn its aberration into lust and licentiousness. All the incarnations of our Lord led a married life and their conjugal relations have been termed spiritual. Our ancient sages suggest that duty, wealth and passion are the steps that lead to salvation. Our moral teachers exhort us to use our wealth for public welfare, expand our love from an individual to the whole humanity and to make everything subservient to the love for divinity.

Our culture advocates a restrained indulgence in sex as the highest ideal of life and as models of happy married life mentions – Shiv-Parvati, Sita-Ram and Radha-Krishna.

We should not turn our back and run away from life but must fully live and enjoy all that it offers. Take passion out of the dirty drain of degeneration and make it a holy step to the temple of refinement. To set forth passion as a virtue lechery is condemned. Portraying a monogamist as chaste and continent shows that if sex life is regulated by piety and contentment it can raise us to spiritual heights. Under the influence of western culture we have renounced this noble ideal. We need not drive passion out of our life but refine and enjoy it with moderation. Then we shall transform the violent force of passion in Godly consciousness.

What Others Say

1. Sexual pleasure, wisely used and not abused, may prove the stimulus and liberator of our finest and most exalted activities. *– Havelock Ellis.*
2. The man experiences the highest unfolding of his creative powers not through asceticism, but through sexual happiness. *– Mathilda Van Kemnitz*
3. There is no greater nor keener pleasure than that of bodily love and none which is more irrational. *– Plato*
4. We are all born for love. It is the principle of existence and its only end. *– Disraeli*
5. Those who have courage to love, should have courage to suffer. *— Anthony Trollope*
6. To fear love is to fear life, and those who fear life are already three parts dead. *– B.A. William Russel*
7. Love is the only glimpse we are permitted of eternity. *– Helen Hayes*
8. There is nothing holier in this life of ours than the first consciousness of love the first fluttering of its silken wings. Love gives itself, it is not bought *– H.W Longfellow.*
9. Of all the qualifications, love is the most important, for if it is strong enough in a man, it forces him to acquire all the rest, and all the rest without it would never be sufficient. *– J. Krishnamurthy*
10. Love is wiser than ambition. *– Barry Cornwall*

Suffering

Life is a sea of sufferings. Pain permeates this whole world. Suffering means mental distress. The feelings that arise in us when we make a mistake, or when others ill-treat us or when our efforts to get success are frustrated cause us misery. There is no one in the world who does not suffer pain of one sort or the other.

How to get rid of pain? The only way is to be oblivious of it. If you turn attention to God you can easily dismiss it. Then you will not only dispel sufferings but also learn how to endure them. You feel pain when you come across detestable objects or situations or part from your dear ones. To ensure happiness, lead an unattached life. It is strange that desire for pleasure always leaves a strain of pain. Often the people feel miserable not because they lack something but because others enjoy it. Endure the pain yourself and share your joy with others and lo! your pain will disappear out of its own accord.

It is a natural fact that man has a tendency to exaggerate and blow up his own suffering and to belittle and scorn even the unbearable and colossal pain of others. The root of pain lies in our aspirations. Some people think that the unfulfilled needs that lie scattered at every step on the path of life cause us pain. But the truth is reverse of it: pain is caused not by needs but by desires, by our covetousness. Those flying high in the sky of aspirations lose contact with the ground realities, which they are ever advised to maintain. Diogenes was content with a tubful of goods whereas Alexander remained discontented though the wealth of the whole world rolled at his feet. It clearly points out that pain resides in the longing that we suffer from while the happiness rises from a sense of contentment. Those who consider destitution a cause of suffering should peep through the window of a rich man's life. If it were the cause of suffering, the rich should be under no stress at all. Irrespective of the material circumstances in which we are placed, pain and suffering, to a large extent depend on our mental attitude. If a man's mind is tranquil like a placid lake it is seldom ruffled by waves of grief and wretchedness which rise when someone disconcerts it with a temptation or allurement.

The mirage of happiness like the blazing desert of pain is only a creation of our own imagination. The scriptures tell us that pain is a constant companion in this journey through the world. Everyone whether rich or poor, grows old and suffers illness. We can absolve ourselves from pain only if we keep our longing for pleasure at arm's length. In the present day world we are not content living within our means but always feel tormented fancying the pleasures our neighbours are enjoying. We are torn by envy and anxiety so much so that we fail to enjoy the simple pleasures of our own life.

If a person crosses over his needs in search of possible pleasures outside, he surely invites pain in his life. A person bewailing of his pain cannot get rid of it; on the contrary he aggravates his distress. Happiness is alike in all people but the cause of pain differs from person to person. A poet has rightly said:

> *"Trudging along these paths*
> *One often runs into the unknown,*
> *But loses those near his heart."*

In attempting to replace pain by pleasure some people go on fretfully complaining about it to all and sundry they came across. The whole world is callous, it feigns sympathy and picks out your suffering, your bitterness and then goes on regaling it to the wide world laughing up their sleeve. This duplicity of behaviour adds to your agony. The real happiness lies in the tranquility of spirit which we wish for but never endeavour to get.

What Others Say

1. God brings men into deep water not to drown them, but to cleanse them. – ***Aughey***
2. Character is formed in the stormy billows of the world.
3. Forgetting trouble is the way to cure it. – ***Latin Proverb***
4. Our strength often increases in proportion to the obstacles which are imposed upon it. – ***Rene Rapin***
5. The greatest griefs are those we cause ourselves. – ***Sophocles***
6. Suffering is the sole origin of consciousness. – ***Fedor Doestoevski***
7. The pain of the mind is worse than the pain of the body. – ***Syrus***
8. Pain to the outcome of sin. – ***Gautam Buddha***
9. The diamond cannot be polished without friction nor the man without trials. – ***Anonymous***
10. Weeping may endure for a night but joy cometh in the morning. – ***Bible***
11. Adversity is the first path to truth. – ***Lord Byron***
12. A wounded deer leaps highest. – ***Emily Dickinson***
13. Trouble is the common denominator of living. It is the great equalizer. – ***Ann Landers***
14. Borrow trouble for yourself, if that's your nature, but don't lend it to your neighbours. – ***Rudyard Kipling***

Anxiety

Anxiety is a frenzy of mind. It is a mental irritation caused by a problem the solution of which is not only baffling but leaves us all the more entangled. Our wise men have defined anxiety as an apprehension about the future, about something that might happen unexpectedly or what lies in store for us. What will this action lead to? When ideas like this throng our mind and make us uneasy and restless, we experience a state of anxiety.

Naturally everyone is anxious for something or the other, but instead of getting non-plussed we can get rid of it if we analyse the problem and try to strike a solution. A rational approach nullifies an anxiety. It has been rightly said that a funeral pyre burns only a dead person but anxiety being more powerful smoulders a living person.

Anxiety is caused by desires, hence the best way to keep ourselves free from anxiety is to restrain our desires. These desires cause sighs of despair. A poet remarks:

> *"Caste away desires and anxiety will disappear;*
> *Control your appetite and you will rule the world."*

The best way to get rid of anxiety is to cultivate the habit of living in the present. Those who enjoy the sight of their expectations projected in the mirror of future should remember that horrible anxiety strangulates all inner good will. Today man is less busy but more perturbed; he lives under the stress of the problem of making both ends meet and failing to find out a satisfactory solution feels more and more bewildered. This anxiety for anxiety's sake lies at the root of all distress. It is no use pruning leaves and branches strike at the stock to fell down the tree. We must be firm in our determination to overcome anxiety, for like termite, it devours the wavering mind.

A man constantly ground in the mill of anxiety has neither peace in the day nor rest at night. He is like an endless caravan of stray thoughts which has neither a guide nor knows the way. The chariot of life moving along the path of anxiety without a guide and a roadmap is not likely to reach its destination. Anxiety prolongs the tale of adversity. Everyone asks the question: What should I do to get rid of anxiety? And the only answer is 'change the direction of your thoughts and ideas'. Overstep your ambition, your desire, your longing and start thinking afresh.

It has been commonly observed that instead of addressing the questions related with his anxiety to himself, a man expects God, or his teacher or his parents to answer them. Their answers might he prompted by sympathy for him but the real solution of the problem lies with him alone. He is like a boy who having misplaced his pencil somewhere in a dark room looks for it in the street outside under a road light. But how can he lay his hand on his pencil until he lights the room.

We must fully involve ourselves in the questions related with our life because the solutions suggested by others are of little help. The solution we ourselves discover is final and effective because we understand the cause of our anxiety better. If we wish to smooth our anxiety over we must find some time for introspection everyday. By smoothing the ruffled feathers you will not only enjoy relief from the scorching anxiety but also steer the boat of your life under a cool shade and then you will realize that the anxiety that appeared like a mountain was nothing bigger than a molehill.

What Others Say

1. It is not work that kills men, it is worry. Worry is rust upon the blade. *– Henry Ward Beecher*

2. Worry can't change the past, but it can ruin the pleasant present. *– Proust*

3. Worry is like a rocking chair. It will give you something to do, but it won't get you any where. *– Church Observer*

4. Don't think of all your anxieties, you'll make yourself ill. *– Shin King*

5. Nothing in life is more remarkable than the unnecessary anxiety which we endure. *– Disraeli*

6. Anxiety is a thin stream of fear trickling through the mind. If encouraged, it cuts a channel into which all other thoughts are drained. *– Arthur Somers Roche.*

7. We have a lot of anxieties, and one canels out another very often. *– Winston Churchill*

8. Worry is the interest paid on trouble before it falls due.

9. Blessed is the person who is too busy to worry in the day time and too sleepy to worry at night. *– Leo Aikman*

Desire

Desires have a world of their own. They are multi-coloured like butterflies. Some desires are clean and healthy and some are dark and morbid. The desires for the welfare of the wider world as well as for philanthropic purposes are auspicious whereas those that serve only self-interest and like a dissembler appear in various disguises are in auspicious and rise from the breeding ground of ill-will, injustice and ignorance.

Generally, a wish to own a particular thing is called a desire. Several desires rise and vanish in our mind every moment. An inert desire is a mere wish. Our desires should not be venomous like snakes but aromatic like the sandalwood that emanates fragrance and provides cool shade. The sea of desires is never quenched; it roars louder and louder as it is filled. To seek fulfillment of your desires, dedicate yourself wholeheartedly to public welfare activities.

Desires are said to be sky high hence the moral teachers advise that they should be such that only our eyes are raised towards the sky, but our feet are firmly planted on the ground. To seek the truth you will have to discard worldly desires which beget only apprehension and anxiety.

Desires are like a fatal disease once they put their noose round a person's neck, it becomes difficult for him to come out of it. As soon as one desire is fulfilled, another arises to take its place. Beginning with the desire for toys in childhood we reach the end of our life's journey when our face is wrinkled, the hair has turned grey, all the limbs have slackened but the desire still rages young and vigorous. The sufferings of one who falls into its venomous clutches begin to multiply like wild weeds. The parasitical creeper (Cassyta filiformis) of desires coils round and round the tree of life and does not release the victim even after it has sapped all its energy. It does not leave even the dead wood but pursues its soul from one birth to another. The journey from one world to another continues till we are caught in the maze of desires, but as soon as we renounce desires our consciousness turns to meditation which drives away all our physical mental and moral ailments and purifies our mind. We recover our health. The day we start thinking about our spiritual welfare, we are back on the right track. The diseases caused by desires and lust disappear. Man does not only regain his mental calm, but also shakes off his physical infirmity.

The source of physical frailty lies in a man's way of thinking. Most of our diseases are caused by our unfulfilled desires which pursue and nag us every moment; not only when we are awake but even during our sleep they appear in colourful dreams. And because of them a man is not at peace during the day nor knows any rest at night. A saint-poet has suggested a simple way of getting rest and peace.

If you wish rest and peace
Move towards the Lord!
Move towards Mammon
If you wish to be noosed.

Desire for rest and peace impels you to seek shelter in God. God's companionship ensures tranquility. But if you wish to live a life of stress and strain involve yourself in the pursuit of money or the worldly pleasures that money can procure. The life of man today is torn by the storms of rage, terror, destitution, ignorance and injustice. And they all are our desires in a disguised and distorted form.

A man should prune his dreams, conciliate his desires but not suppress them because suppression makes them violent and virulent. We should refine them by practising self-discipline and self-purification and exercising restraint in our conduct. Patanjali[1] says that restraint of desire means self-mortification or practising penance that controls the mind roaming freely like a deer in the forest of desires. We should not kill our mind but try to bring it round. Left to itself, the mind is like a child whose tastes and appetites are vacillating every moment. Give him a toy of his choice and the next moment he will demand another. Chastening and chastising would make him rude and impolite. But once he is conciliated and brought round he gives up obstinacy and behaves docilely. If we treat the mind in the same way we shall be playing the role of an enlightened guardian.

What Others Say

1. There are two tragedies in life – one is not to get your heart's desire; the other is to get it. – ***G.B. Shaw***
2. The fewer our wants, the nearer we resemble the gods. – ***Socrates***
3. In moderating, not in satisfying desires, lies peace. – ***Heber***
4. Life is a progress from want to want not from enjoyment to enjoyment. – ***Samuel Johnson***
5. It is much easier to suppress a first desire than to satisfy those that follow. – ***La Rochefoucauld***
6. The more one has, the more one wants. – ***Latin Proverb***
7. The desires of the heart are as crooked as corkscrews. Not to be born is the best for man. – ***W.H. Auden***
8. Life is made up of desires that seem big and vital one minute and little and absurd the next. – ***Alice Caldwell Rice***
9. To have more desire less. – ***Table Talk***

---

1 Patanjali was a grammarian and the author of the *Yoga Sutras* – the earliest treatise on Yoga. He flourished during the second century B.C.

Our Spiritual Wealth

India possesses a wealth before which the wealth of the whole world pales into insignificance. Centuries ago our country discovered meditation. Our saints and sages, thinkers and philosophers tasted the joy of profound meditation or a state of trance. When the world had not yet learnt the first lesson of civilization, the mothers in our country sang this lullaby to their young ones rocking in the cradles: you are part of God who is perfect, wise, pure and formless. When the countries in Europe, Africa and Asia groped into the darkness of ignorance, India was bathing in the brilliance of wisdom. Buddha sat under the Bodhi tree and distributed the light of compassion. Mahavir introduced the philosophy of equality and to his assemblies flocked the men who forgetting the distinction between high and low, rich and poor sat with their companions from the world of birds and animals to listen to his preachings about non-violence, pluralism and non-possession. It is a country where Gita was recited in the battle-field and an atheist like Charvak (pleasant speaker) could be honoured as an Acharya and where Vatsyayana, the author of Kamshastra (Treatise on sex behaviour) could be called a Rishi. All these facts point out a high stage of liberal thinking. Here theoretical differences were resolved through healthy discussions. Here was born Rishi Kanad the scientist seer who taught us the theory of indivisibility of an atom, the harbinger of the modern nuclear age. All the technical terms related with nuclear science are preserved in the Sanskrit language in Vedic literature.

This is the country that taught civilization to the uncivilized and to the civilized it taught culture. It is the country of Patanjali who centuries before the birth of Christ promulgated the philosophy of Yoga and brought out a metaphysical treatise on the Yoga Shastra. It is the country which open-heartedly welcomed all the great ideals that entered from outside and even today welcomes with the same zeal the diplomats as well as ordinary citizens from a neighbouring country which inflicted several wars on us and infringed our boundaries several times.

We always kept the window of our mind open and let the fragrance of Islam drift into our country and settle here. We ordained Christ as Mahatma Isa. The secular country in which we are living today might not have been secular in the modern sense but all the priests of all the communities here emphasized the fact that man is the son of God. We accepted analhaq (I am Brahma) together with monism. The different texts and different sects advocated different modes of worship but the greatness of our spiritual wealth is still a matter of surprise to the modern world. When half-naked Gandhi called for the country's independence he made the most powerful empire in the world tremble with his spiritual power. It is the country that respected the Christian missionaries who entered with a copy of the Bible in their hand. We have borrowed from all cultures and reciprocated them with our wisdom. We never executed a Galileo. We cared for the ideas of even those who despised and disparaged the Vedas, studied their theories together with the Vedic ideals and treated them as noble Aryas. If someone casts a glance at our unfathomable, incomparable and perennial spiritual wealth he will hesitate to call India a poor nation.

It is the land of Khusro and Kabir where Nanak and Farid lived in communion and the Sufis thrived. Here Mira steeped in love for Krishna sang hymns in praise of him. The country gives a call for freedom but uses non-violence as a means to achieve it. The chief feature of satyagraha is its civility. If someone enamoured of material progress of the modern world looks down upon the spiritual wealth of our country, he simply puts a hundred million sons of India to shame.

God

God means supreme authority. He is supreme not because he possesses all the wealth and is the most prosperous but because he is the source, the origin of wealth and is endowed with power of controlling disaster. He creates, sustains and destroys all that we see in the universe.

The invisible power that moves and directs this whole world is called God, Lord of all and Supreme Being. He is associated with our feelings. We may visualize his authority and worship him in any form in which we have faith and belief. We may call him by any name Ishwar, Allah, Wahe Guru or Mahatma Jesus etc, we accept him as the Grand Super human power. Every creature senses his presence, no matter in what form and how long, hence the individual soul being a part of the supreme soul is considered imperishable.

Doubtless, there is a power that regulates this world. God appears both as intangible and tangible. Call sugar by whatever name you please, it always tastes sweet. Similarly, remember God in any form you like he is always benevolent. He never has two opinions and does not discriminate between a theist and an atheist, but showers equal love and grace on all. He has created both the sinner and the meritorious. He is omnipresent and omniscient and an abode of all attributes. For one, who receives his grace all the three worlds[2] are like home. Alas, the individual

---

2 The three worlds are : Devaloka (world of celestials), Manushyaloka (this world of ours) and Narakaloka (hell). The first has nothing but pleasure, the second a mixture of happiness and sorrow while the third has nothing but pain and sorrow.

soul has forgotten God. You will live in God only when you repeat his name with every breath.

Come out of the tanglewood of desires, imagnation and work and find out some time to speak to God. Communion with God, faith in him and repetition of his name never go waste. In this world full of anarchy and chaos, God is the only refuge for the agonized soul. Worship him, serve him and invoke him. Let us feel that he permeates every atom of the world and listen to his dictates. Where there is grace of God, man always enjoys festivity, for sorrow never dare peep there.

We all know that God is omnipresent but conduct ourselves as if he is nowhere. Hence our devotion, our prayer lacks potency. The essence of our devotion and prayer is missing, they are a mere display. Invoke God from your inner soul and he will come and settle in you.

Let us make our heart a temple of God. If we discard all evil thoughts and cultivate only auspicious ones, it pleases God. Those who aspire to propitiate God with an incense stick should remember that God will not be pleased unless the flower of our life blooms and emanates fragrance.

If you love God, everything will come under the sphere of your love and malice will disappear from your life. No one knows when this world cheers and applauds a person and when it pooh-poohs and denounces him. But we constantly receive unbounded love of God and he always accompanies us God lives in all, but no one cares to think of him and this makes for the gloom in their life.

'The best way of worshipping God is to love one and all', advise the holy texts. God listens to prayers that arise from a sincere heart. The glory of God is great. To worship him the sun and the moon burn as lamps, the wind fans a whisk of a yak's tail and flowers offer incense. God has time for the devotees that have time for him, otherwise the sustainer of the creation is very busy. When he withdraws his eye from us everything is topsy-turvy. A poet says:

All boats reach the shore
Also the one without a sailor, rowed by God.

Expressing the same idea, another poet says:

No one can put out the lamp God lights,
For the wind serves as a covering to protect it.

To ensure his personal well-being a man should firmly adhere to one creed, one path, one spiritual guide, one holy book and one God, for we all are but one in the eyes of God, the abode of all deities. Whomsoever we might make an obeisance it reaches that ultimate reality. God protects us all. He is the Supreme guardian. Had he not been so concerned about raising us, he would not have glutted the mother's breast with sweet milk as soon as a child is born. To all the creatures in the whole cosmos he supplies whatever they need.

Soul is God, formless and pure, untainted by birth and death, old age and illness. He is an abode of pure intelligence, bliss and light and eternal source of all wisdom. Such is the nature of God. He sees us all, but we can't and this speaks of our blindness. God is ever ready to shower his grace on us. He is an ocean of compassion. He is kind to us all; it is we who have turned away from him.

The best way to face God is through devotion and dedication to him. Devotion to God means that your mind is steeped in God. Shruti [3] says, God may be master of all but he does not hesitate for a moment to serve his devotee. One who bows to God wins his affection. I bow at his door so that I may not have to bow before others. A poet says:

---

3 Sacred knowledge of the Vedas heard by the rishis and orally transmitted from generation to generation.

The head is not a head
That bows at every door;
And the door where every
Head bows not, is not a door.

We are children of God whether we remember him or not. A son may be good or bad, but the parents are always parents. A man acts but God plays and sports. A man should watch these playful activities of God. God does not expect worship or offerings. He expects people:

- Not to be hostile to any creature, but replete with compassion.
- Not to be attached to material objects, but remain equable in pleasure and pain.
- To be fully dedicated to God.
- Be most submissive mentally and intellectually.
- Not to scorn and reproach others, nor to use a harsh tongue.

Servitude and shamefacedness are closely related. If you leave this world and stand face to face with God without having served humanity you will have to suffer shame. God gave you a face but you have changed it to another. God does not punish you because he wants to seek revenge but because he wants to see you a changed person. God is omnipresent and creates and controls this world through Maya (illusion) as we stand on the ground with a string to control the kite flying high in the sky. It is his play and sport to direct this world. He is not easily accessible and so is his glory.

What Others Say

1. God is our refuge and strength, a very present help in trouble. – ***Bible***

2. God is a circle whose centre is everywhere and whose circumference is no where. – ***Empedocles***

3. The world is charged with the grandeur of God.
   – G. M. Hopkins

4. He is the first and the last, the manifest and the hidden and he knoweth all things. *– Koran*

5. Those who would be children of God must take good heed that their words be simple, clear, truthful and guileless.
   – St. Francis of Sales

6. God's great power is in the gentle breeze, not in the storm *– R.N. Tagore*

7. Conscience is God's presence in man.
   – Emanuel Swedenborg

8. I see God in every human being. *– Mother Teresa*

9. Serving God is doing good to man. *– Benjamin Franklin*

10. God asks no man whether he will accept life. That is not the choice – One must take it. The only choice is how.
    – H.W. Beecher

11. If you begin to live life looking for the God that is all around you, every moment becomes a prayer. *– Frank Bianco*

12. God is like a mirror. The mirror never changes but everybody who looks at it sees something different. *– R.H. Kushner*

13. Prayer is when you talk to God, meditation is when you listen to God. *– Diana Robinson*

Soul

Soul is the centre of Indian philosophical thinking. It is considered an abode of truth, intelligence and bliss which are also the attributes of God, hence the soul is called a shadow of God. God resides in our body as consciousness and this is what we call soul. The body is transient and perishable, but the soul is changeless and immortal. Man's actions in this world determine his next birth. The body dies but not the soul. Soul is a form of Brahma. It is conscious, pure and a fragment of God. Though invisible it watches everything. Man is always apprehensive of an unexpected attack on this body and takes all precaution to evade it, but it is surprising why he doesn't feel pain when his soul is attacked.

Do you not know that your soul is a temple of God? God, in the form of soul resides in you. You should, therefore, squeeze some time to peep inside and see what the soul wants and how best you can fulfil its needs. Steeped in mystic meditation, a Sufi saint laments: 'I and my beloved live in the same street, but alas! We long to meet each other.'

The relationship between body and soul can symbolically be expressed as that between a lamp and its light. The body is a clay lamp and the soul, its light. Soul is immortal and body is a receptacle to hold it. Soul is invisible, imperishable, unsullied and formless whereas body is a gross physical entity but insignificant. Body is a flower, and the soul its scent; body is a journey and the soul, its destination.

We have called soul an abode of truth, intelligence and bliss that is a miniature version of God the supreme abode of these attributes. Hence qualitywise the two don't differ. As a drop and the sea both contain the same water, the only difference being the quantity each holds. The sea is made up of an immense number of drops. As both are the forms of the same element, the one cannot exist without the other. The sea echoes the murmur of drops and the drops dance on the waves. Both have the same nature and share each other's qualities.

It is a law of nature that an element is attracted towards the whole from which it has issued. Light a fire and you will notice that the flames rise upwards because the sun, the source of all fire sits in the sky above. Pour water anywhere, it will always flow in the direction of the sea for that is its source.

The soul may be over-burdened with thousands of entanglements, illusions and infatuations, but it always tries to shake them off and rise above for its final resting place is God. God has created soul, hence it will ultimately merge into him; this assimilation of soul with God is the culmination of its journey through this world.

What Others Say

1. What shall it profit a man, if he shall gain the whole world, and lose his own soul? *– Bible*
2. The soul is the mirror of an indestructible universe. *– G.W.Leibniz*
3. The soul alone raises us to nobility. *– Seneca*
4. As a man casting off worn out garments puts on new ones, so does the soul casting off worn out bodies assumes others that are fresh. *– Bhagwad Gita*
5. There is nothing the body suffers that the soul may not profit by.

6. The wealth of a soul is measured by how much it can feel, its poverty how little. *– W.R. Alger*

7. Death is one of two things. Either it is annihilation, and the dead have no consciousness of anything, or, as we are told, it is really a change; a migration of the soul from this place to another. *– Socrates*

8. The most powerful weapon on earth is the human soul on fire. *– Ferdinand Foch*

9. The soul would have no rainbow had the eyes no tears. *– John Vance Cheney*

10. It is perfectly certain that the soul is immortal and imperishable, and our souls will actually exist in another world. *– Socrates*

Salvation

Before initiating an exposition of salvation, it will be in order to clarify what we mean by bondage. But it is our mental processes that constantly weave out strings that bind our soul. The objective world does not enslave us is our own nature that binds us. So we should try to get rid of these strings; and in this lies our real salvation. Indian philosophy calls salvation by various names such as Nirvana (cessation), Nihshreyas (withdrawal), Moksha (deliverance) and freedom from birth and death. Deliverance consists in freedom from the cycle of birth and death. Man takes several births in this world according to his actions. If we perform good deeds and are devoted to God, we can come out of this cycle of birth and death and get assimilated with the supreme being. It is the state of salvation or deliverance.

The best form of deliverance is deliverance while still living in this world. If you are not able to break the bond while still living, how can you hope to do so after death? Active deliverance means that your actions do not serve only your own self interest but aim at the welfare of all. Renunciation of action is not deliverance, it is simply a way of escape. The real deliverance means acceptance and performance of your duty in the fullest sense. Shruti says: Dispelling ignorance in the light of wisdom, discarding infatuation, love and hate and experiencing uninhibited joy in its own company the soul finds deliverance.

In the centre of the concept of bondage and salvation lies the human mind. Gita holds that only mind is the cause of bondage as well as an instrument of liberation. Nothing binds us to this world – neither house, nor family, nor the members of family.

It is the mind that binds itself to the stake of infatuation. A man can remain liberated while still living in this world and performing all his duties, on the contrary even an ascetic living in the solitude of the forest may bind himself to certain objects. Bondage and salvation do not depend on our circumstances but on our mental attitude. A true devotee does not desire liberation away from this world, but attempts to get it even in the midst of all the material objects of the world. Every religion has seen liberation in the idea of unattachment.

Living as a house-holder one can achieve liberation whereas an ascetic bound in the prison of desires fails to do so. We can get rid of desires only when we see them as bondage because we can never break out of a prison unless we realize that it is a prison. Vivekanand remarks: 'This world is a strange prison-house, here a prisoner does not consider himself a prisoner'. An urdu poet puts the same idea as follows:

O God! bestow on me the wisdom,
and make me see my home as a cage.
Let me not remain a blockhead
that I mistake the cage for my home.

There is no harm if we look upon our home as a prison, but the day we take a prison for our home liberation becomes impossible. We need to change our point of view and as soon as we do that liberation will knock at our door.

What Others Say

1. Human salvation demands the divine disclosure of truth surpassing reason. – ***St. Thomas Acquinas***

2. Three things are necessary for the salvation of man, to know what he ought to believe, to know what he ought to desire and to know what he ought to do.
– ***St.Thomas Aquinas***

Devotion

Devotion means union or conjunction of our inner self with God. We are associated with a number of people but these worldly relations do not fall under devotion. Devotion implies that our soul is tethered to God. A person who faithfully dedicates himself to the service of the Lord is a true devotee. One who is always content, benevolent, is free from arrogance and snobbery and is endowed with a holy nature and a pious personality deserves to be called a devotee.

The devotee sees the reflection of God in everything. For him pleasure and pain, gain and loss, joy and sorrow – all are grace of God. He meditates and concentrates on God whole-heartedly and always sings his praises. The state of mind in which every action of ours becomes a source of joy and happiness, and we get pleasure in serving both humanity and divinity indicates true devotion.

In, the Gita, Lord Krishna proclaims: 'A devotee who is desire-less, pious, efficient, impartial, and above pain and pleasure is very dear to me'. Such a noble devotee sees God in all the living creatures and all the living creatures in God. The so-called devotee of today does not supplicate to God for God's sake, but for some petty objects of sensuous enjoyment. God does not distribute the venom of worldly pleasures but the nectar of union with Him. He deals in gems and jewels, ask him for them and he will shower them on you. If you ask a diamond-dealer to give you coal, how can he fulfil your desire? And it is why a number of people complain that God does not grant their wishes. The fact is that they ask Him to grant them the things which He does not dispense. He is above sensuous pleasures.

A true devotee does not supplicate to God for any material objects, but asks Him to grant him an attitude of detachment, to free him from all desires. He prays to God to restrain his mind from begging worldly objects. When he snaps his relations with worldly pleasures, the devotional service to God begins to take shape in his mind and meditation.

In the Valmiki Ramayana, Ram declares: I do not wish to ask God to grant me a kingdom or the means of pleasure and luxury; if he listens to my devout prayers He may grant me power to relieve people of their distress and wretchedness. When you desire for God Himself your devotion will radiate with efficacy and be a source of strength to you.

If you wish to make your devotion potent and benevolent you must be steeped in God. When you are fully immersed in God your mind will emanate the fragrance of divine bliss or benediction. To experience the presence of God all around is the best achievement for a devotee, but it is possible only when you drive all desires out of your mind. This is true devotion.

What Others Say

1. All is holy where devotion kneels. – ***O.W. Holmes.***

2. To believe in God is to yearn for his existence and furthermore it is to act as if he did exist.
   – ***Miguel De Unamuno.***

3. The devotees who loving me exclusively, constantly think of me and worship me, to such steadfast devotees, I bring full security and personally provide for all their needs.
   – ***Lord Krishna in Gita***

Prayer

The prayer is like an appeal which a human being addresses to the imperceptible God. It serves as a bridge between God and the individual soul; it is a mode of talking to God. In it man invokes God. A true prayer means that one has firm faith in the existence of God and worships and adores him with all his mind, speech and action. We pray to God to grant us success in our undertakings, to protect us from evil and misfortune and to bring about the well-being of mankind.

The form of the prayer when it rises above the level of an individual and is made for the whole humanity becomes more honourable and adorable. God always listens to the prayer made with a sincere heart. So make it a point to remember God in whatever form you like and whenever you find time to do so. Prayer must be genuine and made for some benevolent purpose. Meditation, invocation, adoration, salutation – all are various forms of prayer.

Prayer is not begging; it is an expression of our gratitude to God for what he has bestowed on us. If our prayer is not responded, it means that the way we are soliciting is not appropriate. Instead of praying for material wealth, we should pray for spiritual wealth, persistence and communion with God. This prayer will kindle divinity in us. If you wish to maintain your calm in the face of adversity, then cultivate the habit of saying your prayers regularly. Such a supplicant is granted benediction. A thinker has rightly said, 'If you wish to absolve your inner self from all evil engage in prayer because it is through prayers that one gets the grace of his preceptor and ensures the holy affection of God'. We should address our prayer for the supreme good of the whole creation and not for our personal gains. We need not tell the Lord what constitutes good for us. The object of prayer is to see your personal happiness in the happiness of all. Such a prayer adorns our inner self. O God! I wish to be delightful from the core of my heart. The prayer of those who fail to restrain their mind and purify their heart is meaningless and simply a waste of time. Moving your lips or humming some sounds is not a prayer. When a person prays with his soul and full faith in it, when the prayer emanates from his heart, it directly reaches God. A true prayer means that we cast a glance at our shortcomings, confess our guilt and then solicit God's forgiveness and protection from all the future lapses of character and conduct.

The silent prayers
Promptly reach God
For they are not
Weighed down by words.

How can a prayer rise above words? For this the supplicant must enter a distinctive mental state. The slightest ripple of supplication rising in the heart may better carry away the soul than the long prayer that issues forth from the lips. It is not so important that your hands are folded while you are praying, the important thing is whether your heart is conjoined with God or not. Your voice raised in prayer reaches God only when your heart is with him. An application written on a piece of paper by a student or an employee can secure relief from his daily chore then why can't an application written in heart secure relief from the bonds and entanglements of this world? The only thing you need is to pour your inner self into the prayer. When the inner self, the conscience begins to converse with God, it means that our prayer is meaningful and has accomplished its object.

What Others Say

1. Prayer is conversation with God. – ***Clement of Alexandria***
2. Prayer is the contemplation of the facts of life from the highest point of view. – ***R.W. Emerson***
3. A single grateful thought raised to heaven is the most perfect prayer. – ***G.E. Lessing***
4. Prayer needs no speech. – ***Mahatma Gandhi***
5. Prayer as a means to effect a private end is meaningless and a theft. – ***R.W. Emerson.***
6. Prayer does not change God, but it changes him who prays. – ***S.A. Kierkegaard***
7. If you begin to live life looking for the God that is all around you, every moment becomes a prayer. – ***Frank Bianeo***
8. An hour's contemplation and study of God's creation is better than a year of adoration. – ***Koran***
9. Who rises from prayer a better man, his prayer is answered. – ***George Meredith***
10. Prayer is the voice of faith. – ***Horne***
11. More things are wrought by prayer than this world dreams of. – ***Alfred Tennyson***
12. Our prayers should be blessings in general for God knows best what is good for us. – ***Socrates***
13. Prayer is when you talk to God, meditation is when you listen to God. – ***Diana Robinson***

Incantation

Incantation is repetition of a sacred mantra that helps us cross the ocean of this world. It is the fundamental spiritual observance that successfully rows our boat of life to its destination through all the storms of difficulties and disaster. It bestows on us mental, physical and spiritual happiness and dispels the darkness of distress from our life. Incantation is a process of directing our mind towards God. Repetition of a sacred mantra awakens our soul and even grants us spiritual powers.

A slow continuous chanting of a sacred mantra releases us from the cycle of birth and death and annihilates all our sins. All religions emphasize the efficacy of this repetition as a sure means of realizing the deity. It endows us with mysterious and miraculous powers which strengthen our will power and raise the level of our self-confidence. It crystallizes and sharpens our conscience and makes it more discerning and penetrating. Those who habitually practice chanting the sacred mantra never suffer any kind of physical or mental pain and the sins of their earlier births are annihilated for ever.

Incantation multiplies the joy of life and brings good luck. It gives power to our soul and dispels the darkness of ignorance. Gradually, our infirmities begin to wear down and we become an embodiment of piety and righteousness. Our character brightens and we set out on our journey from deceit and trickery to honesty, from darkness to light, from death to immortality, from depression to hope, from bondage to liberty, from weakness to strength and from malevolence to charity.

Chanting and incantation do not only help the one who practises them but also many others. Everything comes within his reach. It is always beneficial, especially when the mantra repeated is awakened and accomplished in the inner-self.

The mantra for incantation is proffered by an enlightened guru. Only an awakened and sanctified mantra illuminates the soul. It should be repeated with full concentration, affection and devotion. For this the chanter should first listen to the mantra carefully and utter it very accurately with rapt adoration. We have a long tradition of imparting such formulae, but they are of no use unless the guru carefully culls them from a sacred text and ordains life into them.

The mantra may be potent but only a preceptor can infuse force and efficacy into it while teaching it to the chanter. Its light then suffuses the mind and consciousness of the disciple and herein lies the justification for its ordination. By installing the image of a celebrated and accomplished preceptor in his soul, the chanter can visualize the core of the mantra. Like a farmer who prepares the soil in a field before sowing the seeds, the preceptor ordains the disciple so that the living force of the incantation may rise into his inner self. With instructions for the incantation the preceptor installs his wisdom and glory into the heart of the disciple who now sets out on an arduous journey of assent for conquering the summit and bathing in the golden dawn of immovable faith.

What Others Say

1. Incantation is the ultimate weapon of power.

2. Incantation is more eloquent than speech.

Penance

Plainly speaking penance or practice of religious austerity means mortification of the flesh. It is like heating the gold to purify it. A person who does not lose his equipoise in adverse circumstances is called a true practitioner of austerity or an ascetic. Ascetic fervour means that every action must radiate with hard labour. Generally speaking, metaphysics recounts different varieties of religious austerity. For example, austerity of speech consists in naturally and comfortably speaking the truth which is pleasing and useful to all, studying the holy texts with rapt adoration and chanting the name of God. Similarly, practice of good conduct is physical austerity and purity in thoughts and ideas, mental austerity.

Shruti exhorts us to light the lamp of our life with ascetic fervour so that fate may favour us as it favours other lucky ones. Austerity like any other thing such as health or wealth, peace or happiness, family or enjoyment that we get in this world results from the auspicious activities we have practised in reveral births. There activities also arouse in us a desire to consume all our earnings ourselves or to spend them in charity for public welfare.

Everyone aims to attain success in his life and that too without much effort and exertion. But he should clearly understand that no one can ever achieve success just by building castles in the air or without putting his plans into action. Success has to cross the afflictive and distressing valley of assiduous ardour. The object of success whether it belongs to our visible and physical world or the invisible metaphysical world comes from sedulous and strenuous work. Austerity and penance are not means for seeking an escape from the world.

The person, who cheerfully faces the distresses without ever giving up determination to do so, is an ascetic in the true sense. We must cultivate a mental attitude which is at once rigorous and pertinacious as far as our principles are concerned, but affectionate and tender like a flower towards others. A person imbued with ascetic fervour should be resolute and adamant like a rock, but gentle and delicate like a flower.

We often come across people who make a show of austerity, but this hypocricy soon wears off. They can beguile people's feelings only for a short while. We need sincere, selfless and benevolent great men and we must beware of heretic impostors.

We need not dilate on the efficacy of austerity. The religious austerity with which Gandhi ji observed fasts and conducted his Satyagraha overthrew the most powerful British Empire. And it was the austerity practised by our freedom fighters that enabled India to win her freedom. The peaceful followers joined the Satyagraha led by Gandhi ji but those who subscribed to the cult of violence invoked freedom under the leadership of revolutionary ascetics like Bhagat Singh and Subhash Bose.

In short we can say that it is austerity that guides religion, state and society. Without the efforts of resolute ascetics no struggle can be crowned with success.

Righteousness

Dharma or righteousness is what we should hold and live for. It is a perfect combination of our daily routine and moral ideas. To study is the duty of a student and to obey parents that of a son. The duty of a soldier is to defend his country and the duty of a true preceptor is to take the society on the most auspicious path. The duty of a teacher is to impart knowledge and that of a leader to dedicate himself to public welfare. In other words this is their dharma.

Dharma does not indicate a narrow ideology, but a universal and splendid aspect of our life. In our country we don't consider a person religious if he visits the temple and lights a lamp there. For us a person of right conduct who helps the needy is a religious person.

Righteousness comprises all aspects of life. One who is virtuous in all walks of life is a true follower of dharma . But one who observes it only at a holy place is a hypocrite, a dissembler. The one whose whole conduct is imbued with morality can realize the true nature of religion[4]; for him every place whether home or office is a temple of God.

Dharma is a means to salvation. It is universal and indivisible. If one obligatory action obstructs another, it is not the right action but a vicious one. A truly moral action is one which does not block anyone's way. All religions are struggling against immorality. If a religion instigates its followers to oppose those of others it is a slur on the name of religion. We bear the burden of sin in the

4 Religion is not a perfect equivalent of the Sanskrit term dharma, but as it enjoys general acceptance, we have used it here.

name of religion. Can there be any irreligiousness greater than this? Do your duty expected on a particular occasion and in a particular situation religiously and never deviate from the path of righteousness. Religion is basically rooted in humility and brings about salvation, its ultimate goal. Humility helps a man in quickly gaining knowledge and glory and this ultimately leads him to liberation, the supreme objective of human life. A man of virtuous nature does not behave with others in a way which he considers undesirable and harmful for himself. Thus right behaviour is true religion and whosoever performs it deserves to be called a spiritual person. For him all religions are different paths leading to one and the same goal. When our goal is the same, what is the harm if we take any one of the prescribed paths. Today men are wrangling over the paths to be followed. This in no way indicates that religiosity is growing among them.

If we closely examine the conduct of people thronging in religious congregations or bowing their head before the images in a temple we get no inkling that they have grown devout and religious. The people who instigate communal riots and incite people to take resort to rowdism in the name of religion call themselves the custodians of religion. It is strange that those who make holy books and religious texts instruments of creating disturbance in society pretend to raise the banner of religion but do not know how to maintain its glory and honour. The splendour of religion that should permeate the consciousness of the common man has been incarcerated in a temple, a mosque or a Gurudwara. Man reenters into the cloak of his previous malicious self as soon as he steps out of a holy place; precautions must be taken to protect religion from such dissemblers.

Infact, the need of the hour is to save religion from its so-called custodians. The harm they have done to it is far greater than that done by atheists and heretics. Religious teachers are crying hoarse bragging their interpretation of righteousness, but none seems willing to know what human religion is and why humanity is afflicted. If we want to distinguish between what is right and what is wrong we shall have to step down from the domain of mind and convert our heart into a temple by installing true faith in it. And if we really wish to do so the only thing that we need is to practice ourselves what we preach to others.

We must sincerely assimilate in our conduct what we consider right and just. This benevolent view is the mark of a truly righteous person. His divine viewpoint can transform the whole universe into paradise.

What Others Say

1. To die for a religion is easier than to live it absolutely. – ***Jorge Luis Borges***
2. One religion is as true as another. – ***Robert Burton***
3. God builds his temple in the heart on the ruins of churches and religions. – ***R.W. Emerson***
4. He worships God who knows him. – ***Seneca***
5. There is only one religion though there are a hundred versions of it. – ***G. B. Shaw***
6. A good life is the only religion. – ***Thomas Fuller***
7. Religion is nothing else but love of God and man. – ***Albert Einstein***
8. Nothing has made more for peace and charity than religion. – ***Swami Vivekanand***
9. Religion is not a theory of God. It is spiritual consciousness. – ***Dr. S. Radhakrishnan***
10. Religion is the technique of perfect living, of gaining a better mastery over oneself. – ***Swami Chinmayananda***
11. All religions are true, God can be reached by different religions. – ***Sri Rama Krishna***

12. Men never do evil so completely and cheerfully as when they do it from religious conviction. *– Blaise Pascal*

13. There is no religion higher than truth. *– Veda*

14. Religion is morality touched by emotion. *–Matthew Arnold*

15. Every religion is good that teaches man to be good. *– Thomas Paine*

Charity

Charity means 'giving'. Whatever one gives to others is charity. If you expect a return for it then it no longer remains charity but becomes a deal. The charity made to propitiate an angry planet or to ward off a misfortune also falls in this category. It is true that one who gives something gets a return for it, but it should be made to a deserving person. One who gives is great but the one who receives is greater, for the contentment and pleasure he feels in his heart for the donor make him very important. A poet has rightly said:

With sun write the story of shade
And a letter with words of fire,
The recipient reciprocates charity
So put his name among donors.

Charity is the noblest practice that a man should follow and its beauty lies in that the right hand gives and the left remains ignorant of it. The glory of charity lies in that it is given to a meritorious person. It is meaningful only if it fulfils someone's need. Give to a destitute to relieve his poverty. It is useless to give to a rich, for he needs nothing from others and if somebody still gives him he feels no pleasure. Give willingly and not under duress.

If you sincerely give to charity it will release you from the clutches of misery and misfortune. We must give charity for it is said that adversity cannot cross over the wall of charity and it helps in the safe upkeep of wealth assiduously accumulated. People of the world can be put into two classes: those who give and those who receive. Those who receive eat to their fill but those that give have a peaceful sound sleep.

We have no claim over what remains after fulfilling our needs, it rightfully belongs to those who are loitering in poverty and want. Whether we hoard this remainder or squander it over luxuries, we are criminals in the eyes of God. Charity is not just alms giving; it aims at enabling a person to stand on his own feet so that he needs no more help in future and leads a dignified life. If we do so, we are carrying out the dictates of the Lord.

Charity does not reduce our wealth, nay it multiplies it. If you prune the grapevines, they yield more fruit. As soon as charity makes our pocket light, our heart brims with opulence. Whatever we give others, we really give ourselves. If we realize this truth there will be no one who would not like to give charity. It is a law of nature that we should have a charitable disposition. The sun first evaporates the water on the earth and then returns it in the form of rain. We should do the same with our money and wealth.

Indian metaphysics has developed a delightful way of looking at material wealth. It is viewed both as Dhanalaxmi (Stockpiled wealth) and Srilaxmi (Wealth for welfare). The appellation Dhanalaxmi is given by the affluent. It is that part of wealth that is used neither for the individual nor for his family. But when this wealth is used for the poor and the afflicted and the welfare of the world it brings in fame and glory. Then it assumes the form of Srilaxmi and carries the glory of the donor beyond the bonds of time and space. Our nature and attitudes owe their origin to our destiny. Whatever we get is under its dispensation, we are simply an instrument in the hands of the destiny to carry out its will. Then why should we feel excited or arrogant about our acts?

The feeling of vainglory for an act of charity contaminates it. It is like a drop of venom in a jar of nectar which makes whole of the content of the jar deadly. An attitude of insolence and haughtiness mars the whole merit of charity. Someone asked Rahim :

What makes you, O Rahim! Behave so modestly,
The more you give, the meeker you feel?

Rahim replied –

'The real giver is someone else
He keeps filling my coffers
But people presume I'm the giver
Hence I feel abashed.

The one who gives to charity never runs out of money. Shruti says: 'The liberal becomes rich by giving whereas the greedy accumulates wealth but becomes poorer'. Serve mankind silently and let your name be entered in the register of the Lord instead of having it engraved on stone slabs. Charity earns you spiritual wealth. Hoarding money is selfish and immoral; distribute your wealth and rise in the divine estimation.

What Others Say

1. Humility and charity are the two main parts of the spiritual edifice. ***– Rigveda***
2. He who offers good food to the unknown and weary fatigued by a long journey attains to merit. ***– Mahabharata***
3. Riches without charity are nothing worth. They are blessing to him who makes them a blessing to others. ***– Henry Fielding***
4. Every good act is charity. Your smiling in your brother's face is charity. ***– Prophet Mohammad***
5. It is more blessed to give than to receive. ***– Bible***
6. As the purse is emptied, the heart is filled. ***– Victor Hugo***
7. Wealth is meant for charity – giving to the needy. ***– Shankaracharya***

8. True charity never seeks return. – ***Thirukkural***

9. He gives twice who gives promptly. – ***Publilius Syrus***

10. He is rich who hath enough to be charitable.
– ***Sir Thomas Browne***

11. The greatest pleasure I know is to do a good action by stealth and have it found out by accident.
– ***Charles Lamb***

Philanthropy

Philanthropy is a mental disposition which finds expression in behaviour without any conscious effort on our part. It is a natural tendency of human consciousness which raises a person from the level of beast to the summit of ascendancy. In this state he forgets his own self interest and sacrifices himself for the welfare of others. Thus a selfless act done for the good of others falls in the category of philanthropy.

We do so many things in our life. Some of our acts are motivated by self-interest and aim at our personal joy and pleasure while sometimes we do things which aim at the pleasure and well-being of others. To help someone, to compensate for his loss, to express sympathy with a person in distress or providing him financial assistance to redeem him from a difficult situation are all acts of philanthropy. If we are capable and do good to others it is one thing, but even when we ourselves are not in a position to help but persuade someone else to do so, it is an equal act of charity and benevolence.

Philanthropy is the main characteristic of man, it is the simplest way to win fame and glory and prepares ground for his welfare. Anything done for others' welfare earns us merit, so we should be careful not to let any opportunity to do good to others slip from our hands. If a person does not exert himself for the good of others then what is the difference between him and his shadow on the wall. Ancient Indian thought lays stress on the importance of a benevolent and generous act as the surest means of success in life. One whose actions are aimed at others' welfare is considered successful. Fruit-laden trees bend towards the ground, dark clouds saturated with water sag downward, prosperity makes the gentle folk humble and it is an attribute of those who care to do good to others. The following lines by Rahim are very significant:

Trees don't eat their fruits,
Nor do the rivers drink their water,
It is for the good of others
That the wise accumulate wealth!

Charity and not a bracelet adds grace to the hand; similarly, doing good to others and not the physical well-being is the true attribute of a human being. Philanthropy is the true piety hence a man should cultivate and promote feelings of kindness and benevolence in his mind. Goswami Tulsidas says in Ram Charit Manas:

'Doing good to others
Is the best form of piety,
While torturing others,
The vilest form of depravity.'

Benevolence is the best form of religious service whereas torturing and harassing others is the most sinful conduct. A beneficent and generous person is the best creature in the world while ungrateful and unkind, the worst. So tell your children all the good others have done to you and also all that for which you feel obliged to them. Tell them again and again to promote the virtue of philanthropy so that this disposition may pass from one generation to the next and ever expand in the process.

It is a common observation that man speaks very highly of what he has done to others but slights over what others have done to him. Our sages have advised us to exaggerate any little good someone has done to us so that we may feel relieved of the debt we owe him. But today man has completely reversed this notion; he makes a mountain of the tiniest good he has done and decries the immense good others have done to him. This negative approach has obstructed the free flow of benignity in our socity.

Sometimes people fail to do an act of charity though most willing and inclined to do it, for they apprehend some harm might come out of it. We must come forward and make a concerted effort to expand and fortify among people a desire to devote themselves to acts of philanthropy. It will lead to the elevation and progress of the society.

What Others Say

1. If you haven't any charity in your heart, you have the worst kind of heart trouble. – ***Bob Hope***
2. Money giving is a good criterion of a person's mental health. Generous people are rarely mentally ill people. – ***Dr. Karl Menninger***
3. Philanthropy is almost the only virtue which is sufficiently appreciated by mankind. – ***H.D. Thoreau***
4. Philanthropy like charity, must begin at home, from the centre of our sympathies should extend in an ever-widening circle. – ***Charles Lamb***
5. He that hath pity upon the poor lendeth unto the Lord. – ***Proverbs 19:17***
6. Blessed is he who considereth the poor. – ***Psalm 41:1***
7. When thou doest alms, let not thy left hand know what the right hand doeth. – ***Bible***
8. If thou would be perfect, go and sell that thou hast, and give to the poor and thou shalt have treasure in heaven. – ***Bible***
9. Overcoming poverty is not a gesture of charity. It is an act of justice. – ***Nelson Mandela***

Non-violence I

Non-violence is called Paramabrahma – the supreme being. According to Vedanta Brahma is attributeless and intangible Parmatma, who permeates every atom of the creation whether living or non-living. The self attains this state of consciousness when it casts aside dualism and sees everything in itself and itself in everything. Non-violence is equated with this all pervasive Brahma.

For the purification of our consciousness we must get rid of our weaknesses. Similarly, to practise total non-violence in our life we must expand the sphere of our unqualified love for all. Non-violence like Brahma is too fine to be grasped intellectually. It is splendid, formless and expansive like the sky. As soul it exists in all living beings. The followers of non-violence practise it for their own sake. They don't spare the life of an ant for its sake but for their own sake, for their sympathy is universal. Wherever there is pain and distress, it afflicts them. Hence the pain of the ant becomes their pain. During the past thousands of years experiments on non-violence have been performed.

Saint Sane writes: ''Behind non-violence lies a severe penance.'' Large experiments have been made on it. The golden rule that abides in Indian culture from the Vedic period to the present day is this principle of non-violence. All religions, political and social movements in India revolve round this principle. In a way the history of India is a history of experiments with non-violence. A book enumerates 200 examples of such experiments. Gandhi ji says that he discovered non-violence while searching for truth.

He looked upon non-violence as a splendid wealth of the world much above individual penance. However, we can say that no experiment is perfect. Even after thousands of trials; further experiments are being conducted even today, and the concept of non-violence is evolving in a more splendid form.

After Gandhiji, people have presented several formulae of collective non-violence. Vinobaji proposed the concept of 'assimilation of truth' in place of insistence on truth. When we talk about a non-violent society a number of plans arise before us. We think that a non-violent society will be based on the following principles:

1. New experiments will continue to be made for the realization of non-violence.
2. That self-governing society will be complete in itself.
3. It will be fully self-sufficient.
4. There will be no fear of coercion and destructive weapons.
5. Personal property and material possessions will have no value.
6. People will be motivated by service and cooperation.
7. From the national point of view it will prefer labour incentive industries that generate self-sufficiency.

What Others Say

1. Passive resistance is an all-sided sword; it can be used anyhow; it blesses him who uses it and him against whom it is used without drawing a drop of blood; it produces far-reaching results. It never rusts and cannot be stolen. Competition between passive resisters does not exhaust them. The sword of passive resistance does not require a scabbard and one cannot be forcibly dispossessed of it.

   – ***Mahatma Gandhi***

2. The kingdom of heaven is Ahimsa.
3. Non-violence is not a cover for cowardice, but it is the supreme virtue of the brave.
4. There is no such thing as defeat or despair in the dictionary of a man who bases his life on truth and ahimsa.

   – ***Mahatma Gandhi***

5. Non-violence is the first article of my faith. It is also the last article of my creed.
6. Man lives freely only by his readiness to die, if needs be, at the hands of his brother, never by killing him.

   – ***Mahatma Gandhi***

7. Whosoever shall smite thee on the right cheek, turn to him the other also. – ***Bible***

Non-acquisition

Attachment which means the feeling of possessing a certain thing or considering it as your property is acquisition. At the root of this sense of attachment or possession lies desire which impels man to make constant efforts to acquire, hoard and preserve a particular object. In an attempt to establish their control over these external material objects with a view to providing joy and happiness to their people through their consumption even nations have often come to clashes. The problem created by competition for the expansion of trade and acquisition of markets for their products is a fierce one and defies all control. To provide guidance to mankind our saints and seers have discussed in great detail the concept of non-acquisition. The desire to possess a huge pile of material objects like land and property, gold and silver, money and food, servants and retainers etc. is an infringement of the vow of non-possession. Going a step ahead of this infringement thinkers have analyzed the underlying feelings and prescribed restraint of undue indulgence in the senses of touch, taste, smell, sight and speech. The senses must be subdued and restrained.

Indian thought has emphasized the importance of unacquisitiveness in every aspect of life. The Upanishad has commended the path of non-possession and renunciation saying ‘renounce the world and then enjoy it’ and ‘covet not others’ wealth’. Passion, anger and greed are called the gates of hell. The vow of non-acquisitiveness has been proposed to cudgel and crush covetuousness. At the emotional level it has been called contentment and applauded by our sacred texts. The Yoga Shastra includes non-possession among the five forms of continence, and contentment is one of the rules of conduct. Storing for future consumption anything that we don't need today is acquisitiveness.

The one who has immutable and unshakable faith in God Almighty can never support acquisitiveness, for he firmly believes that the God who has given us birth and sustains our life today will continue to do so in future. It is a law of nature that when we really need a particular thing we certainly get it. Hence we need not involve ourselves in unnecessarily storing things we do not need immediately. But it does not mean we should sit idle and do nothing. Even God does not meet the needs of one who in spite of his competence refuses to exert himself and shirks work as if it were a punishment. Those who are unwilling to work can have no faith in God's disposition to take care of the needs of all. Unacquisitiveness does not mean that a person vowed to it should throw away all that he gets or let it go to waste and decay while still living in society. He should take care of every thing as a trustee and should never entertain even for a moment the illusion that he owns it or is its master. He should let people use them if they need them. He who preserves even an old rag against a rainy day for himself or for his offspring and does not let the needy use it is a hoarder.

Acquisition or non-acquisition is a feeling. If an affluent person considers himself merely a trustee of his wealth, he is imbued with a feeling of non-possession whereas a covetuous poor man avid for grabbing whatever he can lay his hands on is actuated by acquisitiveness. We should practise non-acquisitiveness not only at the level of material objects but also at the level of ideas. Some people are dogmatic about their views. Nursing harmful ideas is also mental acquisitiveness. We develop an attachment for whatever we are able to grasp and bring under our sole control and gradually the feeling of possessiveness overpowers us. The true ascetic is one who enjoys supreme bliss though suffering an utter destitution. It has been rightly said:

Dismiss and discard your desire
And worry will leave you carefree;
Restrain your wants
And you'll live like a prince.

What Others Say

1. We are the slaves of objects around us. – ***Goethe***
2. Every increased possession loads us with a new weariness. – ***John Ruskin***
3. How many things I can do without. – ***Socrates***
4. Choose rather to want less, than to have more. – ***Thomas A. Kempis***
5. The more a man possesses over and above what he uses, the more careworn he becomes. – ***G.B. Shaw***
6. The more a man possesses, the more he desires. – ***Proverb***

Fasting

Fasting acts as a stimulant for our self-discipline. It is a form of worshipping as well as a means of controlling our self. It lifts us above our physical senses and places us beside our inner self. It supports our soul and makes us feel its presence very closely.

Literally, fasting (upavas), means 'staying close by', 'to be in the company of', for 'upa' means 'near' and 'vas' means 'to stay,'. If we are nearer to God in thought, word and deed, it is 'upavas' (fasting) in the true sense of the word. Fasting is a discipline which not only purifies our mind but also provides peace and joy to our soul and brings it closer to the presence of God. Fasting also means a vow or a determination. If we discipline our five senses of perception, five organs of action together with mind and are absorbed in meditation of God, the fasting has served its purpose.

Fasting is a powerful means of purification. Human society must give it special consideration, but physical fasting in the absence of mental restraint is a mere hollow display, an act of arrogance and has no meaning.

True fasting means that we should shake off our selfish desires and actions. But today fasting has become a mere hypocrisy. Fasting for getting our trivial demands fulfilled is an affectation, a tactics of exerting pressure. It is a heresy and undermines the sanctity of the term fasting. It must never be associated with demands or it would fall from its high spiritual pedestal. Fasting aims at raising us from the gross level of the body to the spiritual level and when it is above worldliness where do the demands stand? They drop out automatically; there is just a sense of thanks giving. There comes a perception of perfection and thrills us with a feeling of complete fulfilment. Today people are using fasting as a means. From the house wife at home to the people sitting in front of the Prime Minister's House, all are observing fasting with a begging bowl of charter of demands. You must be scoffing if you dare call fasting for demands as Satyagraha. The true Satyagrahi is one who insists on nothing, has no burning desire for any material gain but thinks of the wellbeing of all. He is content with whatever he gets. This is the true import of fasting.

Abstaining from meals is an outer symptom of fasting. Real fasting means that we are not at all concerned with our body and have relegated it to its own care so that we may spend a few moments in the company of our soul. This is the logic behind fasting and one who realizes it is a true follower, a real man of determination.

What Others Say

1. It is easier to abstain than to restrain. – ***French Proverb***
2. The only way for a rich man to be healthy is, by exercise and abstinence, to live as if he were poor.
   – ***Paul Dudle White***
3. To many, total abstinence is easier than perfect moderation. – ***St. Augustine Hippo***

Peace

Waves of ideas keep on issuing in the mind all the time. They always pass through a state of rise and fall. We can achieve mental equilibrium by soothing and pacifying the lake of mind and for this we must learn the art of overcoming indecision. Thoughts like small pebbles cause gyrations of worry and anxiety in the calm lake of mind. When these waves fail to reach the shore we feel agitated and hurt. Then our conscience begins to search for peace and tranquility.

What do we mean by peace? When our mind is unagitated and undisturbed we are at peace. When we are not impatient and restive and are not angry or not thinking of hurting others, we are said to be in a state of peace. From the national point of view we can say that when there are no squabbles and riots, when the difference between the rich and the poor is negligible, when all discharge their duty and are free from the apprehension of war, don't indulge in crimes and lead a contented life, that nation is at peace. Peace is a mental state caused by our auspicious actions and gentle behaviour. If you are as much concerned about the welfare of others as about your own, you'll always enjoy peace of mind. If you think that the difficulties and distress of others are greater than your own, you pave the way for peace in society.

If you achieve internal peace the whole world will appear peaceful. Our peace of mind is disturbed by a craving for what is inaccessible and apathy towards what is available. The key to peace is to be content with what you get and have no ill-will or jealousy towards others. A person who renounces all desires, attachment and arrogance leads a peaceful life. Don't think of wiping anyone out of existence. Live peacefully and let others live peacefully for peace brings about happiness. There is no penance like peace, no happiness like contentment and no affliction greater than desire. And the best form of piety is compassion.

The peace purchased by suppressing problems and quarrels is not peace but armistice, likely to be broken by anyone, any time. Man makes a fundamental mistake when he roams about in search of peace because it is already enshrined in his heart, but man searches it on lake sides and mountain tops, in temples, mosques and gurudwaras. The desire for peace goads him to wander about here and there. You cannot find peace unless you direct your mind in the right direction. In fact, searching it outside is futile. Sit for a moment all by yourself, close your eyes and open the eyes of mind and what you mistook for a dreary desert will appear as an undulating ocean of peace.

To have bodily rest and peace we cease physical work, similarly, for mental peace we should restrain our sense perceptions. We are all the time flipped and thrashed by anxieties, the exhausted body goes to sleep but the mind keeps awake and active to create a world of dreams.

Before going to bed administer this autosuggestion to your mind, 'Today I shall sleep soundly and have no dreams.' Dreams never come true. Even while awake a man daydreams and builds castles in the air. He is never able to break out of this cobweb. Desires not only keep him nagging and pricking while still awake but also tantalize him with wishful dreams during the sleep. In plain language, we can say that he is over-engrossed in fulfilling his wants and desires and in the absence of their satisfaction he can never hope to have peace of mind or to enjoy a state of sublimation.

Try to explore the source of the veiled stream of peace meandering through your mind. But if your mind is always tempted by illusions, you will not find peace even after your death. You may move from one birth to another, but your consciousness will not be able to cast away the coil of strife and discord that grips it fast. A poet says:

You wish for death
When nervous and upset;
Where will you go
If death doesn't give you peace?

Try at this very moment to catch hold of the source of peace. Sustained effort can win all success. Be at ease, regain your calm and search inside you and you'll find the illimitable ocean of peace within.

What Others Say

1. Peace cannot be purchased by compromise with evil or surrender to it. – ***Jawaharlal Nehru***

2. Peace is not in the heart of the carnal man, nor in the man who is devoted to outward things, but in the fervent spiritual man. – ***T.A. Kempis***

3. Peace cannot be kept by force, it can only be achieved by understanding. – ***Albert Einstein***

4. Where there is no peace, there is no limit of suffering. – ***Swami Dayanand***

5. Five enemies of peace inhabit us; viz. avarice, ambition, envy, anger and pride. If those enemies were to be banished, we should infallibly enjoy perpetual peace. – ***Petrarch***

6. Nothing can bring you peace but yourself. – ***Emerson***

7. If we have not peace within ourselves, it is in vain to seek it from outside sources. – ***Rochefoucauld***

8. Those who love and keep peace, preserve the forces of nature – physical, mental and spiritual within themselves. *– Atharvaveda*

9. A mendicant who envies others does not attain peace of mind. There is no happiness higher than peace. *– Dhammapad*

10. Perfect peace can dwell only where all vanity has disappeared. *– Gautam Buddha*

11. The peace found in total self-surrender to God, is altogether pure and spotless, and destroyeth all the troubles mankind endureth. *– Goswami Tulsidas*

12. He who is united with the divine will, enjoys even in this life a perpetual peace. *– St. Alphonsus Lignori*

13. Peace is liberty in tranquility. *– Cicero*

Renunciation

Generally speaking, to renounce means to give up. If we give up our desires, our physical comforts and our evil habits, it is an act of renunciation. Renunciation elevates life and adds excellence to it. Eminence in life is proportional to the extent of renunciation. In the past rishis and munis were adored for they led a life of complete renunciation. Even today we praise, honour and worship those who lead a life of renunciation. A person may renounce his wealth, another his comforts and pastimes and still another may renounce all he has for the sake of public well-being. These are various stages of renunciation. The pleasure we get in renunciation is nobler than that we get in acquisition. The moment we realize the truth of this statement we have taken a step in the direction of renunciation. It is suggested that we should make a beginning with the renunciation of our attitudes. It is a well-attested fact that change in the attitude will certainly bring about a change in our nature. Give up pride and everyone will love you; give up anger and your distress will disappear and if you give up greed you will enjoy bliss. Renunciation is a potential step in the direction of truthfulness.

Renunciation means surrendering everything for the sake of truth. If renunciation makes you arrogant it is not true renunciation, for renunciation brings about peace. Hence renunciation of egoism is real renunciation. Renunciation does not mean that you wear coarse clothes, spurn your body or eat dry crumbs of bread. Renunciation means overcoming your wish, curbing your fancy and crushing your longing. Renunciation means driving the disposition out of mind that drags you into the whirlpool of arrogance. Renunciation is meaningless until you get rid of pride and self-assertion. We often see people adopt such behaviour in the name of renunciation which has no inkling of renunciation in it. Strange are the ways of haughtiness. The pride brought about by renunciation is harmful. Arrogance caused by desire may be dispelled with renunciation, but the conceit generated by renunciation challenges both learning and consciousness of man polluting thereby even the sublime thought of renunciation. The course of one's life who has a distorted structure of thinking never runs smooth.

In a moment of renunciation a man is so attuned that he is ever ready even to sacrifice his life for the sake of fulfilling his mission. Renunciation is indeed a strange temperament; it prevailed on Rama to accept banishment, on Buddha and Mahavir to relinquish their kingdoms for the life of an ascetic. It was this disposition that converted Mohandas Karamchand into Mahatma Gandhi and inspired Bhagat Singh with indomitable patriotism and courage to sacrifice himself for the independence of India and be known as the greatest martyr.

Renunciation fills us with a supernal power. This sentiment is incomparable. It wants unflinching dedication towards its objective. Unfortunately, there are only a few who willingly undergo all tortures and pass through the flames of five without wincing an inch from their determination. Even the celestial pleasures cannot tempt them to deviate from the path of renunciation. The tales of paragons of renunciation who, charitable by nature, never went back on their word adorn the pages of history. The temperament of such adherents of self-abnegation is as much responsible for holding the world in its place as the axis on which the earth moves. Hindu mythology has it that the earth rests on the hood of Sheshnage[5], the symbol of renunciation who bears the load of earth on its head to carry out the wish of the Lord.

5 Shesanaga, also called Ananta, is the thousand-headed cosmic serpent. His head sustains the earth. Vishnu reclines on the coiled form of Sheshanaga

Saint

A saint who represents intangible God on this earth in physical form is adorned with the attributes of eternity and infinity. To realize this eternal authority of a saint we must comprehend his nature. A self-effacing person who makes constant efforts for the wellbeing of others is called a saint. A person who has conquered desire and envy, is always imbued with the idea of God, is extremely patient and unassuming is entitled to sainthood. His heart is soft and tender as butter and is always generous and benevolent by nature. He lives not only for himself but for the whole creation as well and provides shelter to the suffering humanity. His company is joyful and beneficial. He is as sacred as a place of pilgrimage. Praising a saint Kabir says:

Moon is not cool, nor snow
Saint is the coolest who loves all.

A saint may profess to any religion but his heart always brims with the same love, the difference that we see between various saints is imputed by us; it is our own creation. The one who robs is a robber and the one who sacrifices everything for the world is a saint. To lighten everyone's heart, the saints have lighted the torch on every path. Hence the saint is often compared to the sun which gives light to one and all without any discrimination. The saint is impartial and free from all encumbrances and inspires the whole atmosphere with benignancy.

A saint subdues his senses and rises above infirmities. Aristotle says that a saint is always on the move but his mind is stable whereas the mind of a householder who generally stays at one place knows no constancy. The saint does not restrain his mind but withdraws it from sense objects and the one who exercises control over his mind can hope to understand the world. The teachings of a saint have great potency. They can change the condition and direction of our life. A saint is known by his actions and not by his cowels.

There is a perfect coordination between what a saint preaches and what he practises. His outer conduct reflects his ideology. He is always considerate about others' wellbeing. In his eyes he nurses the dreams for others. He does not dream for himself because for him the world itself is a dream, an illusion. His life is a confluence of the Ganga of divine knowledge the Yamuna of right conduct and the Saraswati of good manners joining together to form one stream. Such saints have always guided and led the human society. Whenever the atmosphere in the world has been vitiated by suffering and sinfulness, strife and discord, the saints have shown the way out by their life and message.

The saint is a bridge that brings together all the castes and communities in which our society is divided. He binds all the humanity into one integrated whole. He is a messenger of God and sacrifices his life to create a divinely unified society. Such saints have cleansed the stream of our culture by carefully sifting all the impurities and rubbish that has accumulated over the years and contaminated it. Our country will always remember such saints with respect. We are indebted to them.

What Others Say

1. Some rivers pass through others without mingling with them, just so should a saint pass through the world.

   – Ralph Venning

2. Sainthood emerges when you can listen to someone's tale of woe and not respond with a description of your own.

   – Andrew V. Hason.

3. When I give food to the poor they call me a saint.

   – Helder Comara

4. There is a land of pure delight; where saints immortal reign. ***– Isaac Walts.***

Abstinence

Abstinence denotes the principle of moderation in life. A flying bird maintains its balance on its two wings, a moving cart balances its weight on its two wheels and the dancing nature sustains itself on the cycle of seasons. Similarly, abstemiousness plays the same role in the life of man, it facilitates his journey in this world. We may be placed in any circumstances whatsoever; they will not affect our mental poise till we exercise self-control. We can master the art of controlling our mind by observing rules of conduct meant to keep us wakeful and watchful.

Our commitment to rules disciplines us and provides a key to success in life. The man who is disciplined in his food and drink, his conduct and deportment and character is certain to achieve his goal in life. His body is free from ailment, mind filled with unending joy and he lives in a world of divine happiness. A disciplined life is a fountainhead of energy. Look at the life of a disciplined soldier and a self-controlled saint and you will notice a queer rhythm in them. The font of immense energy that sustains the life of a saint and a soldier has its source in their life style which is regulated under strict discipline.

A bridge joins the two banks of a river. Similarly, the bridge of self-control connects the outer and inner life of a man and propels and stimulates his progress on the path of life. Observance of even minor rules of life makes for self-reliance. The rules may appear minor and inconsequential but they have great power. They make our life well-ordered. Unfortunately, at present man leads an irregular life which makes him less busy but more disturbed. When we learn the technique of putting every second to its proper use we shall feel a strange vigour sprouting in us. To generate vigour and vitality and to strengthen the force of our character we must resolve to exercise self-control. It will add dignity to our life and keep us within proper bonds. Uncontrolled and unprincipled life style destroys our peace of mind and pushes the boat of our life into the storm of stress.

Indian metaphysics compares human life to a vast ocean embanked by dignity to confine it within bounds. If you peep through the window of people's life you will see that most of them are torn by anxiety and smouldering in the fire of distress and destitution. The basic cause of all this is their intemperate life.

Abstinence means a principled and well-balanced life. The Sanskrit equivalent of abstinence is 'Samyam' where the prefix 'Sam' means systematic, planned, correct, and 'Yam', 'control'. Hence, 'Samyam' is the right type of control, a discerning self-discipline. It is a rightful regulation of our energy and makes it blossom forth in creativity. It generates a benevolent desire in our consciousness and helps lead a qualitative life.

Come, let's resolve to practise moderation in every aspect of our life. If we lead a principled life governed by self-control we shall move on the road to eternal bliss. If we fail to do so we shall not be able to live in harmony with nature. By establishing harmony with nature we can experience self-realization and meditate on God. This is the highest goal of our life and for it alone we live.

What Others Say

1. There are two ways to live your life. One is as though nothing is a miracle. The other is as though everything is a miracle. – ***Albert Einstein***
2. You will go most safely in the middle. – ***Ovid***
3. Moderation in all things. – ***Terence***

4. A responsible man needs only to practise moderation to find happiness. – ***Goethe***
5. He will always be a slave who does not know how to live upon a little. – ***Horace***
6. In everything, the middle course is the best, all things in excess bring trouble to men. – ***Plantus Possy***
7. It is better to rise from life as from a banquet, neither thirsty nor drunken. – ***Aristotle***
8. Moderation is the silken string running through the pearl chain of all virtues. – ***B.P. Hallf***
9. Moderation is the centre wherein all philosophies, both human and divine, meet. – ***Hall***
10. Temperance is the lawful gratification of natural and healthy appetite. – ***J.B. Gough***
11. Moderation is the secret of survival. – ***Proverb***
12. Even moderation ought not be practised to excess. – ***Anonymous***
13. Moderation in temper is always a virtue. – ***Thomas Paine***

Virtue

Virtue means moral excellence that improves our life in this world as well as in the next. A meritorious act is a sacred and benign undertaking whose performance brings us joy, satisfaction and peace. A virtuous act is motivated by a desire to do good to every creature. Indeed any act considered just and reasonable by the standards of the family and the community and which wins applause not only for itself but for the doer also is a virtuous act. It earns merit in this as well as in the next world.

Whenever we get an opportunity in life we must do as many benevolent acts as we possibly can. A man is certainly rewarded for his virtuous acts but he should not expect it for virtue is its own reward. A virtuous act may not bring any material gain but it develops a courteous disposition whereas a sinful act results not in poverty but in malicious temperament. A desire to do a kind and charitable act brings in wealth. If only hard labour had made man rich, then why are most of the labourers poor? Similarly, if only intelligence had brought in riches then why are wise men always hankering after it?

Opulence follows meritorious acts and those who perform them are always rewarded. The easiest way of performing a virtuous act is to repeat the name of God because forgetting it is the vilest omission. Every one is born with closed fists but leaves this world empty-handed. He is advised to make an effort, so that he leaves the world with his hands full. And for this he should perform meritorious acts as well as seek blessings from the saints. Whenever an opportunity calls for a benevolent act be quick on the draw to throw yourself into doing it. Those who procrastinate should remember that our breaths are numbered and nobody knows which one may be the last. Our sages have advised that man should accumulate wealth and wisdom as if he were immortal and imperishable but while performing religious or meritorious acts he should remember only that death may come any moment without warning hence he must embark on meritorious acts without wasting any time. If we perform benevolent acts with this intent our life will not be accursed with any sin.

We earn merit from charitable acts. Our deeds must be pure and pious. If our thinking is imbued with truth, clarity and simplicity our acts will be just and righteous and bring in good reward. If we unite our senses and mind with beneficial actions we shall be generating merit every moment whereas the one who yokes his temperament to evil actions will always face malevolent and baleful circumstances.

We must develop a favourable disposition towards one and all for the journey towards gain begins with auspiciousness. Merit results from the accumulated benevolent actions performed in the past life and it is rewarded with fulfilment of desires, success and prosperity in this life. Let us lead an auspicious life at present so that our life in the next birth might be happy and meritorious. If we cultivate good manners we become entitled to a happy, successful and meaningful life.

What Others Say

1. Five things constitute perfect virtue – gravity, magnanimity, sincerity, earnestness and kindness.
2. Virtue is a kind of health, and good habit of the soul.

   – ***Plato***
3. There is no road or ready way to virtue.

   – ***Sir Thomas Browne***

4. A thankful heart is the parent of all virtues. – ***A Proverb***

5. The happiness of man, as well as his dignity, consists in virtue. – ***John Adams***

6. The essence of greatness is the perception that virtue is enough . – ***R.W. Emerson***

7. It is virtue, and not birth, that makes us whole. Great actions speak great minds, and such should govern. – ***John Fletcher***

8. Virtue is the denial of self and response to what is right and proper. – ***Confucious***

9. God likes him who leads a virtuous life. O Lord make us virtuous. – ***Rigveda***

10. He is ill-clothed that is bare of virtue.– ***Benjamin Franklin***

11. Courage is the ladder on which all the other virtues mount. – ***Clare Boothe Luce***

12. Virtue does not come from money, but from virtue comes money and all other good things to man, both to the individual and to the state. – ***Socrates***

13. Good company and good discourse are the very sinews of virtue. – ***Izaak Walton***

14. Virtue is the font whence honour springs. – ***Christopher Marlowe***

15. The one and only true nobility is virtue. – ***Juvenal***

16. Virtue is better than immortality and life. Kingdoms, sons, glory, wealth all these do not equal one sixteenth part of the value of virtue. – ***Mahabharata***

Concentration

The steadying flame of the lamp, the bee settling on a flower and the carefree moth circling the candle light are all examples of concentration. When you compare various resolves, consider all the alternatives before reaching a conclusion, it is concentration. Technically, we can define concentration as the unflagging devotion to our goal. We must devote heart and soul to the goal we have set before us and should not relax till we have realized it. This steady effort is possible only through concentration and for this we need to control our mind which in itself requires specific skill. We need concentration of mind as well as of our point of view. To achieve a higher goal we need to sacrifice minor interests. This sense of renunciation comes from concentration alone.

The most sensible thing that we can do in life is to concentrate our energies and the worst is to squander them. A sage has remarked, 'When I concentrate on a spiritual issue I am not distracted by anything worldly.' How can we make ourselves useful? Address this question to yourself and the answer will be self-evident and most probably it will be negative. Then what should we do? A thinker suggests: 'Direct your attention and energy to the things you are interested in and don't deviate from the rational course.' Be what the nature wants you to be and the sweet smell of success will greet you. But if you go against it you will not achieve much. The truth of this dictate can be realized through concentration. When we centralize our ideas on a point it is the beginning of concentration. We can put the same thing in a slightly different way. We talk of first concentrating our mind but this seems to be an almost insurmountable problem. Even the most accomplished saint finds it difficult to concentrate his ideas. All our scriptures are of one mind about the intractability of controlling our mind and advise us to make an attempt in this direction by degrees.

If you wish to reach the top floor of a ten-storey high building you must climb step by step. It is impracticable even to think of reaching there in a jiffy. For this we shall have to go step by step resting our foot on each stair and make a sustained and untiring effort till we reach the top. A poet says:

When darkness fills a room
Keep a candle lighted
And keep on the spirits,
For the dawn is at hand.

The same holds true of concentration. We must move on step by step. First let us learn how to concentrate our body. It can be done by controlling our posture. Then we must control our breath. Pranayam helps us here. Next we should hold our tongue, for silence is golden. After it we should try to concentrate our mind that is our thought processes and ideas. We will notice that when our body, breath and tongue make a rhythmic movement we move closer to the window of our mind. And when the mind begins to make a rhythmic movement too, the whole body becomes attuned to its purpose, our mental capriciousness disappears and an all-round harmony emerges. Our mind will begin to stay at one place and all hesitation or vacillation will cease. This is a state of steady concentration. The point where our ideas converge is the moment of supreme concentration for our consciousness.

What Others Say

1. Concentration is the secret of strength in politics, in war, in trade, in short in all the management of human affairs. *– Emerson*

2. A man's judgement is best when he can forget himself and any reputation he may have acquired and can concentrate wholly on making the right decision. *– Raymond A. Spruance*

3. Concentration is my motto – first honesty, then industry, then concentration. *– Andrew Carnegie*

Mind

Mind is very playful and unsteady. Like a naughty and frolicsome child it wants to hop and jump, rise and fall. The agility with which mind goes up and comes down and creates confusion and disorder in ideas is incomparable with anything in the world. Mind is at the back of all our experiences, our actions and the inspirations that we feel. Mind gives birth to ideas and turns people into our friends or enemies. It is the mind that governs all the functions our body performs, hence we should exercise control over it. We can check its fickleness by directing it to the services of the Lord, singing hymns, spending time in the company of religious people and by exercising rules of conduct and restraint.

We should discipline our mind so that the sense organs that are controlled by it function properly.

Being fickle and inconstant by nature it creates turbulence in the life of man. It is difficult to hold back air, but it is still more difficult to control mind. It is like a pampered child who is always demanding one thing or the other. Instead of coddling our mind we must restrain and regulate it. One who has conquered his mind has subdued the whole world. We can't keep away from love and hate until we discipline our mind which is a slave to senses and habits. To elevate your mind remember the formula; Narrow-mindedness makes you poor, but open-mindedness makes you rich.

Controlling mind is like controlling a car running at full speed. It is foolish to press the accelerator and wish to stop the car, for this you should raise your foot from the accelerator and put it on the brake, both the accelerator and the brake are close by to make it easy to operate them with one foot. If you wish to keep the vehicle of your mind on the right track you must maintain a balance between the acceleration and the brake. If you keep on pressing the brake for too long it will bring the vehicle to a standstill, but if you keep your foot on the accelerator, the speed may go out of your control and endanger your life.

The best thing is to make a proper use of both the accelerator and the brake. This applies to mind also. We should neither allow it to run unrestrained nor retard it so much that it makes no progress at all.

Mind is too tender to be killed, it must be understood. To kill mind is violent but to bring it round needs great sensitiveness and compassion. Those who advise us to crush the mind are neither rational nor pious. We must keep it steeped in good thoughts, which will help elevate it. To think of crushing the mind is a negative approach. Instead of creating vacuum in the mind make it creative, involve it in some constructive activities and then it will generate a new revolution which will change not only your point of view but also the whole creation. One who has mastered the secret of mind's working can understand the whole world. He gets rid of all confusion, progresses every moment and is a truly advanced person.

What Others Say

1. Our mind is like a garden, which can either be intelligently cultivated or be allowed to run wild.
   – R.K. Murti
2. Minds are like parachutes, they only function when open. ***– Thomas Robert Dewar***
3. When the mind is free, the body is delicate.
   – Shakespeare

4. Riches, fame and pleasure, with these three, the mind is so engrossed that it can hardly think of any other good. ***– Baruch Spinoza***
5. Your prayer must be that you have a sound mind in a sound body. ***– Juvenal***
6. On earth there is nothing great but man, in man there is nothing great but mind. ***– Sir William Hamilton***
7. Great minds have purpose, others have wishes, little minds are tamed and subdued by misfortune, but great minds rise above them. ***– W. Irving***
8. The mind is said to be two-fold
   The pure and also the impure
   Impure by connection with desire
   Purity separation from desire. ***– Maitri Upanishad***
9. A good mind is a lord of a kingdom.
10. Strength is a matter of the made up mind. ***– John Beecher***
11. A vacant mind is open to all suggestions, as a hollow mountain sectors all sounds. ***– Chinese Proverb***
12. The mind is like the stomach. It is not how much you put into it that counts, but how much it digests. ***– Albert Jay Nock***
13. A cup is useful only when it is empty, and a mind that is filled with beliefs, with dogmas, with assertions, with quotations is really an uncreative mind. ***– J.Krishnamurti***
14. People have the strength to overcome their bodies. Their beauty is in their minds. ***– Peter Gabriel Clark Brown***
15. A man's mind is steady when he withdraws his senses from sense objects as the tortoise its limbs from all sides. ***– Bhagavad Gita***

Moral Sayings

Moral sayings are the maxims that light the dark path of our life and guide us. They came from the great men who acted on them in their life before codifying them as moral principles. Thus these moral sayings or holy precepts summarized on the basis of ripened knowledge and experience are meant to enable us to keep on the right track in our life.

These moral sayings never grow old and outdated nor are they biased and unfair. They are pure and holy like the Ganga water and give us happiness and eternal peace for several births. They are like the nectar and act as elixir both for the body and the mind.

While elaborating moral sayings or explaining their esoteric connotation care should be taken about the selection of the right audience lest they might be misused to harm you. If you sincerely act on the moral sayings you will become a cultured and a noble man. Hence these sayings and exhortations ought not only be read but understood and acted on.

The treasure house of our culture, literature and folk lore contains numerous pearls and jewels of moral sayings which are culturally more valuable than even gold and silver. These matchless golden words are much above the precious stones. A man can realize their efficacy only by assimilating them in his conduct. These days when we glance at the morning newspaper we see reports of murder, violence, rape, theft, robbery and other heinous crimes. The events that are telecast live are ominous. Giani Jail Singh, the former president of India said that he began his morning reading moral aphorisms from Gurwani, the Gita and the Bible and read the newspaper during the siesta. So his morning was well-begun and if the morning is auspicious the whole day is auspicious.

A man should start his morning with reading the scriptures. It is like a dip in the Ganga that washes away dirt that soils our mind. It will help us keep our conduct ethical during the day. Every child in the country should do so to learn the moral principles. To fill your room with the light of inspiration you may get down some moral truths on a piece of paper and hang it in your room.

What Others Say

1. Morality is not properly the doctrine of how we may make ourselves happy, but how we may make ourselves worthy of happiness. – ***Immanuel Kant***

2. All sects are different because they came from man, morality is every where the same because it comes from God. – ***F.M. Voltaire***

3. What is moral is what you feel good after, and what is immoral is what you feel bad after. – ***Ernest Hemingway***

4. We must conform to a certain extent to the conventionalities of society, for they are the ripened results of a varied and long experience. – ***A.A. Hodge***

5. It is easier to fight for one's principles than to live up to them. – ***Alfred Adler***

6. Expedients are for the hour but principles are for the ages. – ***H.W. Beecher***

7. Act only on that maxim which you can at the same time wish that it should become a universal law. – ***Immanuel Kant***

8. The three hardest tasks in the world are neither physical feats, nor intellectual achievements, but moral acts to return love for hate, to include the excluded and to say. I was wrong. – ***Sydney J. Harris***

9. Moral excellence comes about as a result of habit. We become just by doing just acts, temperate by doing temperate acts, brave by doing brave acts. – ***Aristotle***

10. The biggest threat to our well-being is the absence of moral clarity and purpose. – ***Rick Shuman***

11. The glory of great men should always be measured by the means they have used to acquire it.
– ***La Roche Foucauld***

Fate

Fate or destiny rules the life of man. It is difficult to unravel the mystery of human fate. Destiny is unpredictable, it occurs without any previous intimation. Defining destiny it has been said that whatever man gets in his present life as a result of the accumulated actions performed in the previous birth is called his destiny.

Unfortunately, sometimes even a gentle person is seen leading a miserable life while the lucky ones enjoy all pleasures of life though devoid of any talent. With his action, enterprise and luck a man can transform even adversity into most prosperous circumstances. For this, a man must be brave and adventurous. Scriptures tell us that God helps those who help themselves. Destiny obeys those who row the boat of life with sails of hard work. Look at this saying: whatever a man is destined to get, he will get it even in a desert and nothing more than that even if he comes on a heap of gold. So we should not be rapacious. A jar will contain only that much water as it has capacity to hold whether we fill it at a well or a sea.

Fate is determined by a combination of competence and manliness because it favours only those who help themselves. You cannot decide your luck unless you make full preparation and invest all your effort. Money obeys a truly lucky person, but the luckless is a slave of money. Those who live in the present build their fate. It is said: Bury the dead past, the boundless future lies ahead and remember each word, idea and action builds your luck. In our life we must be cautious about things that drag us towards misfortune. A wise man learns what to avoid from the misfortune of others.

We must understand the obstacles that lie scattered on the way of unlocking our fate otherwise we shall fail to visualize many dimensions of fate. Our knowledge helps us in overcoming obstacles. If instead of reproving fate we muster all our force and fortitude and push the chariot of life it will not only run smoothly but success will finally greet us. If you just sit idly hoping for, fate will never smile on you and you will be disappointed.

The favourites of fortune are those who toil doggedly from dawn to dusk. The true devotees of the goddess of fate are those whose forehead glistens with drops of sweat. There is a proverb that a sleeping lion starves while an active prowling cat feasts on milk and cream. The goddess of fate embraces the hardworking man. We cannot achieve anything meaningful in the absence of labour.

Fate is a naughty phenomenon and must be trusted as much as a naughty child. We may sing praises of fate but those who sit idle cannot hope to brighten their future. A poet has rightly said:

What can luck do if there is no labour?
And what can labour do if there is no luck?

If labour and luck join hands they can bring about a revolutionary change in the life of a person. Labour or luck alone fail to achieve much.

What Others Say

1. My view is that to sit back and let fate play its hand out and never influence it is not the way man was meant to operate. – ***John Glenn***
2. Sow an act, and you reap a habit. Sow a habit, and you reap a character. Sow a character and you reap a destiny. – ***Charles Reade***
3. How a person masters his fate is more important than what his fate is? – ***Wilhen Von Humboldt***

4. There is no armour against fate. *– James Shirley*
5. We make our fortunes and we call them fate. *– Disraeli*
6. Destiny has two ways of crushing us by refusing our wishes and by fulfilling them. *– Henri Amiel*
7. Prepare for the worst, expect the best and take what comes. This is fatalism. *– Anon*
8. A man's character is his fate. *– Heraclitus*
9. I claim not to have controlled events, but confess plainly that events have controlled me. *– Abraham Lincoln*
10. For man is man and master of his fate. *– Alfred Lord Tennyson*

Thought

Man has a power to think which gives him dignity and justifies his appellation as man. Man is endowed with rationality which has enabled him to raise and organize society and lies at the root of the concept of nation and citizenship of the world. Thinking is a mental process performed by human mind. The thoughts and notions that grow as a result of thinking are called ideas. A man's talent and ability is judged by the way be preserves his ideas and expresses them through speech and conduct.

Our thoughts and actions must be healthy so that they elevate not only our character but also stimulate the welfare of others. Like a puff of wind good thoughts should be expressed at the right time. Thinking good thoughts is not enough, we should also put these thoughts in practice. The indigested ideas are as harmful as indigested food, however, the latter may be cured but the former adversely affects our manners. The thoughts that have not been translated into action, howsoever noble, are like the scattered pearls. Through our conduct we can string them into a necklace.

There is nothing either good or bad in the world but thinking makes it so. Our inadvertant behaviour is responsible for half the mistakes committed by us. We act rationally where we should be emotional and vice versa. Great thoughts when put into action give birth to great deeds. Deprived of the light of ideas, the conduct is blind. Those who have noble thoughts are never alone. Noble thoughts are like flowers but acting on them is stringing them into a wreath. You should nurse in your mind only the thoughts that your inner consciousness, your intelligence and your heart like and support.

Don't cram your mind with useless information. Forget trivialities to make room for divine ideas. Neither let your mind lie idle nor dump meaningless rubbish into it. Our conduct depends on noble ideas but if we don't act on them they are no better than inert fanciful dreams. Think of what you want to be.

If we are considered important because of our high office, then it means that we are not really great in any way; it is the office that is important.

If money makes us important then money and not we are important. Mind always roams in the world of ideas. Thoughts come and go but in passing they leave an indelible mark on the life of man. Let us keep our ideas ever fresh. When we are obdurate about a particular idea it means that we have lost our flexibility and freshness. Prejudice and stubbornness are like evil planets which adversely affect human life.

It is a maxim that only the dead and the fool cannot change their ideas. Predisposition and obduracy are stumbling blocks in the way of healthy growth of ideas. We must entertain the living ideas and discard the dead and outdated ones. When the mind is tired the flow of ideas ceases. Flowing water is clean, so let your ideas flow, let them progress. Don't think that by changing your ideas you will deviate from your principles. Ideas determine the principles but when the process is reversed man falls a victim to stupidity and lifelessness. Support the living and not the deceased.

Ideas supported by principles and truth will fill your inner self with eternal light. Ruminate on your ideas and you will realize the truth as you get butter by churning the milk. Always keep this fact in mind and your life will become lively and fragrant like a garden in the paradise.

What Others Say

1. As he thinketh in heart, so is he. – ***Proverb***
2. Any man may make a mistake, none but a fool will stick to it. Second thoughts are best, as the proverb says. – ***Cicero***
3. Great thoughts reduced to practice become great acts. – ***William Hazlitt***
4. They are never alone that are accompanied with noble thoughts. – ***Philip Sidney***
5. You are today where your thoughts have brought you, you will be tomorrow where your thoughts take you. – ***James Allen***
6. To think is to live. – ***M.T.Cicero***
7. It is the hardest thing in the world to be a good thinker, without being good self-examiner. – ***Shaftsbury***
8. Sooner or later, false thinking brings wrong conduct. – ***Julian Huxley***
9. Our life is what our thoughts make it. – ***Marcus Aurelius***
10. Great thoughts come from the heart. – ***Marquis De Vanvenargues***
11. Thought is the soul of act. – ***Browning***
12. Thought takes man out of servitude. – ***Emerson***
13. Thought without action is an abortion, action without thought is folly. – ***Jawaharlal Nehru***
14. All the actions that we see in the world, all the movements in human society, all the works that we have around us, are simply the display of thought, the manifestation of the will of man. – ***Swami Vivekananda***

Present

The simplest definition of present is the moment in which we are living. Time is an indivisible unit and cannot be divided into segments. Man is endowed with imagination so what has been over he calls past and what is yet to come, future. The interlude between them, the moment currently passing is the present in which we live our life. The moment that has been spent has become a part of the past and the future is yet unborn. The journey of life passes through these three periods. The childhood passes in the present, the old age moves about in the experiences of the past and the youth peeps into the mirror of future.

Let us explain it in some detail. A child always lives in the present and is happy; he has nothing to worry about the past or the future. The youth are not so much concerned with the present but are busy weaving dreams about the future. The old always talk about their past. They live in the world of past experiences and enjoy talking about them. In a way they draw sustenance from what has been past. These three divisions of life represent the three periods of time.

What is happening now, the occurrences today make our present. It is our knowledge about the present that enables us to think about our past or future, but what is past is past and there is no use thinking about it, and what lies in store in future depends on the will of God. So all our actions both secular and religious are performed in the present. If we neglect or forget the present we cannot plan a bright future. So our present is very important and before deciding on an action, we should carefully think over it. One who is indifferent to his present loses everything. Ten thousand past 'yesterdays' cannot equal one 'today.' Shruti says what you want to do, do it now in the present with faith in God and confidence in yourself. You should not grieve over what is past because grief kills patience. You should also not worry about what is likely to happen in the future. The wise and intelligent devote their heart and soul to make their present a success. We should improve our present and enjoy it fully. If we make a good use of our present for our wellbeing, we sow the seeds for even better future. If you take care of the present, it will take care of everything, but if you worry about the past and future you lose everything. A man must live in the present to lead a happy, healthy and pure life. Those who live in the experiences of the past complain against the present and those who dream about the future grow discontent with the present. To live in the present is the real way of living. Future is unborn, the past is dead, only the present is living hence a man should strike a favourable balance with the present.

The one who enjoys his present to the full can hope for a better future and can make the past interesting. What is present today will tomorrow change into the past. To make his life meaningful one should live in the present and utilize every moment of it. One who moves with the present is up to date and progressive. Think and plan for the present only, do today what you want to do without worrying about the past or future. Then only your life will be worth living and enjoying.

What Others Say

1. All the treasures of earth cannot bring back one lost moment. *– French proverb*
2. Tomorrow's life is too late. Live today. *– Martial*
3. Happy the man, and happy he alone,
He, who can call today his own :
He who, secure within can say,
Tomorrow do thy worst, for I have lived today.
– John Dryden

4. We want to live in the present, and the only history that is worth a tinker's dawn is the history we make today.
   – Henry Ford

5. Every situation no, every moment is of infinite worth for it is the representative of a whole eternity. ***– Goethe***

6. Seize the day, and put the least possible trust in tomorrow. ***– Horace***

7. Every present joy or sorrow seems the chief.
   – Shakespeare

8. Every man's life lies within the present; for the past is spent and done with, and the future is uncertain.
   – Marcus Aurolius

9. Look upon everyday as the whole life, nor merely as a section, and enjoy and improve the present without wishing through haste, to rush on to another.
   – Jean Paul Richter

10. Let not the mistakes of yesterday, nor the fear of tomorrow spoil the day. ***– Calton Everett Knox***

11. Trust no future, however pleasant!
    Let the dead past bury its dead!
    Act-act in the living present!
    Heart within and God o'er head! ***– H.W. Longfellow***

12. Whatever you can do, or dream you can, begin it. Boldness has genius, power and magic in it. Begin it now. ***– Goethe***

13. The present is the point at which time touches eternity.
    – C.S. Lewis

14. Whoever doesn't know the past must have little understanding of the present and no vision of the future. ***– Joseph S. Raymond***

15. Learn from yesterday, live for today, hope for tomorrow.

16. Science is knowledge. Wisdom is knowledge tempered with judgement. ***– Lord Ritchie Calder***

17. Knowledge helps you make a living; wisdom helps you make a life. ***– Sandra Cave***

Yoga

Yoga is not only the root of all the ascetic penances but the est form of ascetic practice also. Our mythology tells us a story that Shukdeva, the son of Vyas was born as a bird in a previous birth and listened to the discourse of Yoga from the mouth of Lord Shiva himself. This transformed him into a renowned yogi in the next birth. It means that the practice of yoga will bring you celestial joy and bliss and fulfil all your wishes and desires. The scriptures hold that overwhelmed by ignorance the soul became the individual self subjected to three forms of pain and suffering physical, mental and spiritual. The only way of deliverance from them lies in the practice of yoga.

Without the practice of yoga we cannot understand the illusory play of nature because it is only a yogi whom the nature fails to tempt and entrap. It becomes nervous in his presence and takes to its heels. In simple words we can say that a yogi vibrates with a natural rhythm and no longer remains an individual self but becomes part of the eternal truth. And it is because of this quality that yoga is considered the best form of ascetic practice.

All the religions in the world follow, in one way or the other the path of yoga. The mantra of the tantaric system, the Allah of Islam and the Jesus of Christianity may differ from one another but when their followers are steeped in meditation they unknowingly enter into the world of yoga. Even then the scriptures of no religion except that of the Aryans describe and support the culmination of all rituals in the yoga. Whatever be the liturgical practices in other communities in India all forms of prayer and worship are based on yoga. When through the practice of yoga you concentrate your mind, it generates wisdom that releases the human soul from bondage. Nothing else can give you this wisdom. Bhagwan Shankar Dev holds that the study of hundreds of books on logic and grammar makes a man engrossed in academic distinctions and confused. In fact no one can gain true wisdom without practising yoga. Through an intense study the yogis have sucked the essence of all the four Vedas and other scriptures and the rest of the academicians are just scrambling over the left over. The Yogis have churned out the butter and the others are destined to be content with butter milk alone. The knowledge gained from a study of religious scriptures may be a confused babbling. It is not the true knowledge. When we withdraw our mind, intellect and sense organs that are directed towards external objects and turn them towards the inner self and merge into God Almighty we get true wisdom. When a man gets rid of all the worries and anxieties and the mind is in a fluid state, it is called yoga. Yoga also means the cessation of mental functions or modifications of mind through which the self knows the objects of the world. These changing states and processes of mind find expression in three states of wakefulness, sleep and dream. The mind always tries to get rid of these modifications and regain its original form but the sense objects drag it outside. To suppress and terminate the senses to enable the mind to have self-consciousness or the experience of the transcendent spirit is called yoga. If the mind is not cleansed it cannot be restrained. It is like a dirty piece of cloth that does not take a colour unless it is washed clean before dying in another colour. If the water in a pond is dirty and turbulent we cannot see its bottom. We can see it only when the water is clean and calm. The bottom of the pond is our real self. The pond is the mind and the movement of its water is its modifications. Why can't we see the transcendental spirit sheltered inside us? Our mind is dirty because of sins like violence and disturbed by processes like hope. If by an observance of restraint and rules of conduct we wash away the dirtiness of mind and restrain the mental processes it is yoga.

By observing ascetic practices like the rules of conduct and principles we can get rid of sins such as violence, desire and greed etc. and restrain the free flow of mental modifications activated by desires and passions and realize the supreme consciousness established in our heart. After this realization the illusion between mine and yours disappears. We comprehend the true nature of the world, the family and children and attachment to gold or iron. Steadfast devotion and universal love rise in our heart.

There are four kinds of yoga – Mantra yoga, Hatha yoga, Laya yoga and Raja yoga but at present it has become almost impossible to practise Mantra yoga and acquire perfection in it. When the mind, while chanting a mantra, fully immerses into itself, it is called Mantra yoga. Without understanding the esoteric meaning of the chant and full dedication while repeating it, the Mantra yoga is not realized. Then there is no right type of guide to initiate into this practice which requires a continuous preparation over several births to realize it.

Hatha yoga is also beyond attempt and realization. The symptoms of Hatha yoga are as follows:

The word Hatha is a compound of 'ha' (the sun) and 'tha' (the moon). Apan Vayu (the wind released by human body) is called the moon and the Pran Vayu (the life breath) is called the sun. So a conjunction of Apan Vayu and Pran Vayu is Hatha yoga. The conditions conducive to Hatha yoga and the body to stand the practices are rare in the world today.

Raja yoga, though free from dualism is very painful for the people today. Moreover, in the absence of practical demonstration, the Raja yoga is impossible to imbibe through a study of books. For the people in our age whose life span is very short and who suffer from malnutrition Laya yoga has been recommended as easy and comfortable. It has several varieties. Everything internal or external that we can think of may be instrumental in the practice of Laya yoga. We can concentrate our mind on any object and get fully absorbed into it to accomplish 'Laya yoga'. Thus the practice of yoga fills every moment of life with joy and enthusiasm.

What Others Say

1. Equipoise is said to be yoga. Also equivision is yoga. Yoga is adeptness in work too. – ***Bhagavad Gita***

2. Yoga is getting to God, relating ourself to the power that rules the universe touching the absolute. It is the yoking not merely this or that power of the soul, but all the forces of heart, mind and will to God.
– ***Dr. S. Radhakrishnan.***

Knowledge

Knowledge is the end product of the process of knowing. In man's physical and spiritual development knowledge plays the same role as the eyes play in his life. Life is meaningless without eyes and without the eyes of knowledge it becomes insubstantial and worthless.

Any type of spiritual, literary or artistic skill and information is called knowledge. A knowledgeable person is one who knows everything worth knowing. In our day to day conversation we say 'He has a very good knowledge of the language' or 'that he is familiar with the fine nuances of music' or 'that he is adept in a particular field'. Thus knowledge consists in having special information about a particular field and the person who has accumulated all this information in detail and depth is a scholar, a wise man or a savant.

The person who has spiritual knowledge is known as an accomplished seer or an erudite. Knowledge like the ocean is vast and expansive and knows no bounds. The society honours all the three – the knowledge, the knower and the knowable. Knowledge is a double-edged sword. If the purpose of attaining knowledge is not auspicious it becomes a curse, a sin. Our knowledge should find an expression in our conduct because the light of wisdom radiates from the heart of one who acts on what he says to tell others. Wisdom enters the inner space from where the darkness has been dispelled and God settles there.

Wisdom is a true mirror. If one goes on expanding his knowledge in a particular field he becomes aware of his ignorance in it.

And it is the true knowledge that makes the life of a wise man unique and amazing. The wise man smilingly enjoys the world whereas a fool is always wailing and whining. A foolish person is devoid of knowledge but full of egoism caused by ignorance. It makes him presume that ego itself is knowledge. Similarly, the arrogance caused by the possession of knowledge is the greatest ignorance.

It is easy to make an ignorant person wise but it is next to impossible to impart knowledge to one who is arrogant and misapprehends ignorance for knowledge. Knowledge does not mean simply a collection of information. It must awaken our consciousness so that we may understand ourselves both at external and internal levels. Information introduces us to the external world but wisdom opens a view of inner-self. Wisdom is compared to a lamp placed on the threshold, which lights the house both inside and outside. Similarly, wisdom throws light on the external world of experience as well as the inner world of ideas. We cannot comprehend the whole of our life without lighting the world of ideas. Our practical life in the external world cannot be auspicious in the absence of knowledge of the inner-self.

A truly wise man does not only read the book of life but assimilates the wisdom that pervades its pages and moulds his conduct accordingly. If our wisdom does not find an expression in our conduct the blessing of knowledge changes into the curse of arrogance. The knowledge that does not stand the test of purity in the laboratory of life causes indigestion. The wisdom that does not form part of life remains a conceit of speech and creates embarrassment for us. But a day comes when the lamp of knowledge of the one who rises above false and illusory platitudes becomes a sun and lights the whole world.

What Others Say

1. Knowledge is power. *– Hobbes*
2. The knowledge which purifies the mind and heart alone is true knowledge; all else is only a negation of knowledge. *– Sri Ramakrishna*
3. Knowledge comes, but wisdom lingers. *– Tennyson*
4. Knowledge is proud that he has learned So much, wisdom is humble that he knows no more. *– Cowper*
5. All information is not knowledge; all knowledge is not wisdom. *– Anonymous*
6. A king is honoured only within his own bounds, a learned man is respected everywhere. Knowledge is a great wealth. It cannot be shared by kinsmen, or stolen by thieves; it remains intact though given away to others. *– Chanakya*
7. To know one's ignorance is the best part of knowledge. *– Lao Tse*
8. He who knows others is learned. He who knows himself is wise. *– Lao Tse*
9. Knowledge cannot spring up by any other means, than enquiry, just as the perception of things is impossible without light. *– Shankaracharya*
10. The person who knows everything has the most to learn.
11. Strange how much you've got to know before you know how little you know.
12. As we acquire more knowledge, things do not become more comprehensible, but more mysterious. *– Albert Schweitzer*

Coexistence

Coexistence is the foundation of creation. A number of social problems that crop up as a result of neglecting the principle of coexistence can only be solved by reviving that principle. Nature has ordained things in a way that all the animate and inanimate creatures in the world depend on each other. For their birth, their up-bringing and their security all human beings depend on others in one way or the other. This mutual interdependence is co-existence. Man being endowed with intelligence enjoys the highest place in the creation and by expanding and regulating this principle of coexistence he organized society.

If it had not been so man would have remained an animal because no single person can fulfil all his needs. To procure food for his body he might take to agriculture and might keep cattle to get milk but it is not possible for him to manufacture cars, aeroplanes, T.V. and fridge etc. all by himself. He cannot be an engineer and a doctor at the same time. Even to do a single thing he has to draw on the help and cooperation of others.

If a person devotes all his time and energy to scientific research he needs others to help meet his other needs. Someone grows food for him and someone weaves cloth. Division of labour and mutual cooperation have enabled man to lead a comfortable and organized life. Thus besides his individual existence a man has a social existence as well. It is why the progress of society depends on the progress of the individual and vice versa.

Unfortunately, the society is growing more and more narrow-minded these days. We have become so individualistic that for our small gain we do not hesitate to cause the greatest damage to others not sparing even the society and the nation. Some people stoop so low as to eliminate their political or business rivals. Incidents of murder among the students because of academic competitions have come to light. The tendency to encroach upon public property is on the rise. We feel insecure and apprehensive in the society which earlier looked after our safety and security. Even trusted close associates are seen getting their companions involved and engrossed in criminal cases. Is it not our responsibility to work for mutual social security? We neglect our social responsibilities and in consequence suffer in various ways. Children fear to come out of their house to play openly in their street and colony. This sense of insecurity forces us to get our children admitted in expensive residential schools. Attending day schools has become risky. Students have no faith in their classmates. Unruly elements and goons are exploiting the rich in the name of providing them security. Is our social indifference not responsible for all this? We ourselves are responsible for creating this undesirable situation in society. When a stranger meets an accident on the road, we are reluctant to take him to hospital little remembering that accidents have become common and we are often alone outside. If we care for the safety and security of our neighbour it ensures our own safety and security. It is our little actions that make the social atmosphere pleasant or unpleasant.

A man is indebted not only to his parents and teachers but also to society. In a way to a large extent the former is a part of the latter. When we borrow money, goods or services from others we should not forget to repay them. Our sages and seers, scholars and philosophers have bequeathed us an invaluable treasure house of wisdom, science and literature which we are making use of in various ways. It is also a debt that the society owes to them and we keep on reminding ourselves of it from time to time when at the death of a celebrity or a literary scholar we say that the society will ever remain indebted to him. If we redeem this pledge, then a number of problems will be resolved automatically. In other words, we can say that we should clearly recognize our responsibility to the society and try to fulfil it. Besides this we should try to contribute something fresh to the best of our ability to the society without thinking what the society gives us in return. Directly and indirectly we have taken a lot from the society and still continue to do so. We should give something in return also. Society owes its existence to this kind of replenishment.

What Others Say

1. You can't run a society or cope with its problems if people are not held accountable for what they do.
   – John Leo
2. Both optimists and pessimists contribute to our society. The optimist invents the airplane and the pessimist the parachute. ***– Gil Stern***
3. To live in society does not mean simply living side by side with others in a more or less close cohesion, it means living through one another and for one another.
   – Paul Eugene Roy
4. Civilization is a process whose purpose is to combine single human individuals and after that families, and then races, peoples and nations, into one great unity, the unity of mankind. ***– Sigmund Freud***
5. We ought to think we are one of the leaves of a tree, and the tree is all humanity. We cannot live without the others, without the tree. ***– Pablo Casals***
6. No one is rich enough to do without a neighbour.
   – Harold Helfer
7. Man seeketh in society comfort, use and protection.
   – Francis Bacon
8. The pillars of truth, and the pillars of freedom, are the pillars of society. ***– Henrik Ibsen***

Guru's Grace

Guru's grace means that a person is surrounded by energy and as soon as he opens the window of his heart it flows into and fills it with the feelings of veneration and makes his inner self vibrate with thanks giving. The stream of his thought stops for a moment with a sudden shock. In other words we can say that it forges a connection between the power of that Splendid Being and your inner self. The Splendid Being is a treasure house of boundless energy of which you need only a small fraction to light your life. When that source of all energy touches your consciousness you are surprised and filled with energy. Anything might happen when the energy of guru's grace flows, it may light your lamp or it may burn it. If the inner consciousness is not capable of holding that energy it would upset whole cycle of life, but if it is able to hold it, it opens many hidden dimensions of consciousness. Osho says that the direct transmission of energy into you is hazardous hence it is better to let it enter your inner consciousness through the agency of a guru, a teacher who acts as a regulator, as a transformer. He estimates your capacity and releases only that much of energy flow into you that you can absorb and assimilate in your consciousness and saves you from possible hazards. Hence, the agency of the guru is essential. Guru bears and holds the flow of that infinite energy and slowly passes it on to you.

The contribution of a Guru is that he consecrates and prepares you but it does not mean he gives you an amulet, a charm or a necklace to wear. He delivers knowledge and wisdom and dispels the illusion of distrust that fills your inner-self. Thus consecration means passing through the process of absorption of energy that begins when your self-consciousness comes in contact with the Eternal source of energy. How does it happen? Kabir says: Only he that has burnt his hut can follow him. With this initiation and preparation, the guru turns the flow of our energy towards the Lord. Compared to the Lord who is a diamond, desires are stone and who is there in the world who would like to go in for a piece of stone when he has already found the diamond? Guru's grace changes our mental make up, fills us with a unique energy and the change becomes visible in every aspect of our life. This transformation brings about a self-revolution.

What Others Say

1. A master can tell you what he expects of you. A teacher, though, awakens your own expectations.
   – Patricia Neal
2. A great teacher never strives to explain his vision, he simply invites you to stand beside him and see for yourself. ***– Rev. R. Inman***
3. To teach is to learn twice. ***– Joseph Joubert***
4. When you teach your son, you teach your son's son.
   – The Talmud
5. The work will teach you how to do it.
   – Estonian Proverb
6. If you would thoroughly know anything, teach it to others. ***– Edwards***
7. No one was ever really taught by another; each of us has to teach himself. ***– Swami Vivekananda***
8. One good school master is worth a thousand priests.
   – R.G. Ingersoll
9. Nobody can be taught faster than he can learn.
   – Samuel Johnson

10. A teacher affects eternally, he can never tell where his influence stops. – ***Henry Adams***

11. The true aim of everyone who aspires to be a teacher should not be to impart his own opinions, but kindle minds. – ***F.W. Robertson***

12. True teaching is not that which gives knowledge but that which stimulates pupils to gain it. – ***Milton Gregory***

13. You cannot teach a man anything you can only help him to find it within himself. – ***Galileo***

The Journey of Sanskars

Psychology tells us that our mind has two divisions: conscious and unconscious. All our good and bad experiences of the past are stored in our unconscious mind. A malicious action might leave a deep scar in our heart and we begin to nurse feelings of revenge against its author. These feelings culminate in the complex of enmity which gets firmly implanted in the unconscious mind.

In childhood our unconscious mind is a clean slate. The teachings and sanskars imparted by our family and elementary teachers are indelibly inscribed on it. It is difficult to obliterate them. They serve the important role of a foundation for the edifice of our personality. In this period the clean slate of unconscious mind is protected by our family, our parents and primary teachers. The conscious mind undergoes changes in the present environment that surrounds us. With his bitter experiences, sometimes, the unconscious mind cautions the conscious mind. All our notions about sin, merit, hate, enmity, compassion, kindness, affection, love, devotion and asceticism are stocked in the unconscious mind. Innumerable floppies recording our various pleasant attractions, deep wounds of suffering, undesirable behaviour, hate, malice, insult and love lie stuffed in this chest. Sometimes the conscious mind takes an action after due consultation with the unconscious mind. The unconscious mind is a placid pond in which our conscious mind takes a holy dip after completing the journey of repentance. In this pilgrimage our self obviates its separation from the world. Dirty sewage water flowing in a drain merges into the Ganga and becomes holy like it. Similarly, the impure mind surrenders to the holy self and merges with it. As a result of this merger the complexes long settled in the unconscious mind disappear and the mind becomes one with the consciousness. It gets rid of all desires and assumes the form of self. The saints and seers of yore engaged ascetic practices disdainful of the enjoyment of the superficial beauty of the ephemeral world to explore the eternal beauty lying encrusted with it. They very well knew that the enjoyment of the superficial beauty might yield a temporary pleasure but will ultimately land them into bitter and violent pain. So they assiduously endeavoured to enter into the depths of the physical beauty. They discarded the outwardly beauty and turned their mind to the inner beauty of the self.

This journey towards internal beauty was a move in the direction of the spirit and was later on termed spiritualism, that is the movement of mind extracted from the worldly pleasures and illusions towards the spirit to surrender to it. The false illusory network of worldly pleasures and luxuries has been compared by the Upanishads to a golden bowl covering the truth of the supreme soul. This golden bowl obstructs the view of the truth that permeates the physical world. We should adorn our unconscious mind with lovely images of sanskars so that we might contribute our share to the organization of a noble and virtuous society.

Words

Words have a world of their own. They define the whole universe. In the absence of words no religion and philosophy, science and literature, history and culture would have come into existence. The whole knowledge is contained and codified in words. Words are at the back of all genres of the world. They are the basis of our speech.

The use of words may give us pleasure or pain. Their value and significance lies in their use. To express your idea in the fewest possible words is an art because like the treasure of Aladin there are several hidden treasures that can be opened with the key of words. The words once uttered never come back. Regulated use of well-thought out words expresses the seriousness of the speaker's nature.

Words are colourful and concoct strange images. One word enters the soul of a man as a drop of nectar whereas the other is poured through the ears as a draught of bitter poison. Words have immense power. They put a man on the path of either development or destruction. Words are responsible for the rise or fall of a civilization. They are the bridges that connect man's ideas with the physical world. Had there been no words man would have remained uncivilized. When the ideas of man find expression through words they create civilization.

Our scriptures also discuss the power of words. Words have their origin in sound and reveal the world, hence they are called Brahma. The words are Brahma hence their power is Maya (illusion). When they create doubt and illusion they manifest their illusory power to deceive man. The relation between words and truth is weakening and wearing away at present. Words must be worshipped as Brahma and used sparingly because the superfluous and meaningless words create confusion. Information technology has widened the scope of word all over the world. Print and electronic media have done injustice to words and lowered their dignity.

The soul of a word lies in its meaning but today man uses soulless words which make life complicated. Words should be used to express the truth, if they are used to tell a lie, they make our life burdensome.

Weigh your words on the balance of reason to see whether the pan holding the truth is lower or the one holding the lie and you will yourself see whether you have made a meaningful use of words or not. If the words are sincere and meaningful they boost the success and progress of a business but if they are false and meaningless they harm your reputation and shatter your public image. Think carefully before you speak out and you will find that your words are not less potent than chants or sacred formulae. Sweet words please you and win your affection but unpleasant words deserve to be forgotten. The use of balanced and truthful words is an accomplishment. One who uses few friendly and benevolent words is a finished person.

What Others Say

1. A very great part of the mischiefs that vex the world arises from words. – ***Burke***
2. Words should be scattered like seeds, no matter how small the seed may be, if it has once found favourable ground, it unfolds its strength. – ***Seneca***
3. In the beginning was the word, and the word was with God, and the word was God. – ***Bible***

4. Words are like leaves, and where they most abound, much fruit of sense beneath is seldom found.
   – Alexander Pope

5. A blow with a word strikes deeper than a blow with a sword. ***– Robert Burton***

6. Words are what hold society together. ***– Stuart Chase***

7. Men of few words are the best men. ***– Shakespeare***

8. Good words are worth much and cost little.
   – George Herbert

9. It is with a word as with an arrow once let loose and it does not return. ***– Abd-el-Kader***

10. That bath knowledge spareth his words. ***– Proverb***

11. Sharp words make more wounds than surgeons can heal.

12. A single word often betrays a great design.
    – Jean Baptiste Racine

13. Words are vehicles that can transport us from the drab sands to the dazzling stars. ***– M. Robert Syme***

14. Words of comfort, skilfully administered are the oldest therapy known to man. ***– Louis Nizer***

15. The most valuable of all talents is that of never using two words when one will do. ***– Thomas Jefferson***

16. Never answer an angry word with an angry word. It's the second one that makes the quarrel. ***– W.A. Nauce***

17. By this words thou shalt be justified, and by thy words thou shalt be condemned. ***– Bible***

Virtue

Excellent life-values of a man make him virtuous. A virtue is an attribute that acts as the best bridge between the nature and a person's attitude. Virtue means excellence also. Auspicious acts are considered good and inauspicious, evil. Although man is a bundle of slips and errors, yet everyone is endowed with some good quality. The special trait that impresses others or wins their appreciation is called the quality of that person. The person who possesses a number of qualities is admired by one and all. Some of these qualities are innate and some are acquired. Sweet tongue is an innate quality but the propensity to respect and appreciate others is an acquired habit. The best quality that a person is expected to have is the acceptance of everything that is good and benevolent and avoidance of what is wicked and malevolent. Both the qualities as well as the person who possesses them are admired everywhere, but a man of quality is advised not to keep silent otherwise no one would know about his qualities.

There are only a very few persons in the world who feel pleased at heart and appreciate even the smallest quality that others have. On the other hand the number of those who make a mountain of the molehill of others' faults but overlook their own Himalayan blunders is far greater. It is very difficult to acquire these four qualities: piety with wealth, modesty with charity, compassion with bravery and humility with authority. We must explore the virtues of others and try to acquire them ourselves. Unfortunately, most of us make a mistake here: instead of ever trying to learn something from others, we are content with simply appreciating their qualities. The better approach would be to acquire these qualities ourselves.

Shruti says, 'If you sow the seeds of virtue in your family, they will multiply.' Discuss good qualities, enjoy, adopt and make them a part of your life. The expansion of virtue expresses through our conduct in three ways – we think good, speak good, and do good. One who is rational and well-mannered acquires many virtues. Truth and auspicious ideas find expression in his speech like the shower of the Nyctanthes blooms. A man of wicked nature emits negative energy wherever he sits. Negative thinking, negative conversation and negative body language mark his conduct. Even a single person with negative attitude contaminates the whole atmosphere.

A question arises here: How can we make ourselves virtuous? The simple answer is: Regulate your life. At present management has become the talk of the town. We constantly hear of home management, office management and management of every aspect of life such as family, society and nation. But man is oblivious of the management of his own self and this is responsible for the present chaos in our life. A person solicitous about his life management can develop good qualities and make his life a garden of colourful and fragrant flowers of virtue. A man endowed with virtue should never expect praise from others. We are mentally ruffled both by praise and reproach. We should sing in praise of God alone and never flatter others nor expect flattery from others. If we respect good qualities we should adopt them in ourselves and then every particle in nature will glow with light of inspiration.

Learn from the flowers
How to smile
And from the bees how to sing.
Learn from the fruit – laden branches
How to meekly bow your head.

A person always eager to adopt good qualities makes his life charming and his real self finds expression in the virtues he possesses. Impress others with your good qualities and not with your physique. One who possesses good qualities is a thousand times superior to the one who is only physically attractive, nay he is far above the beautiful, the rich and the wise. A man of virtue is respected everywhere is an old saying. If we wish to cultivate virtue we should be well-mannered and be on the look out for noble qualities. If we are able to do so our life will disseminate sweet swell like a flower.

What Others Say

1. The happiness of man, as well as his dignity, consists in virtue. – ***John Adams***
2. What doth the Lord require of thee but to do justly, and to love mercy, and to walk humbly with thy God. – ***Bible***
3. The souls of the righteous are in the hand of God, and there shall no torment touch them. – ***Bible***
4. There is no road or ready way to virtue. – ***Thomas Browne***
5. The humblest citizen of all the land, when clad in the armour of a righteous cause, is stronger than all the hosts of error. – ***William Jennings Bryan***
6. The essence of greatness is the perception that virtue is enough. – ***Ralph Waldo Emerson***
7. Virtue is harder to be got than knowledge of the world; and if lost in a young man, is seldom recovered. – ***John Locke***
8. Virtue may be assailed, but never hurt, surprised by unjust force, but not enthralled. – ***John Milton***
9. Do good by stealth, and blush to find its fame. – ***Alexander Pope***
10. Charms strike the sight, but merit wins the soul. – ***Alexander Pope***

11. He lives in fame that died in virtuous cause*Shakespeare*
12. Nothing can harm a good man, either in life or after death. *– Socrates*
13. Virtue consists not in abstaining from vice, but not desiring it. *– Bernard Shaw*
14. It is virtue, and not birth, that makes us noble. Great actions speak great minds and such should govern. *– John Fletcher*
15. Virtue is the denial of self and response to what is right and proper. *– Confucius*
16. Good company and good discourse are the very sinews of virtue.
17. All bow to virtue and then walk away. *– De Fenod*
18. Fivethingsconstituteperfectvirtue:gravity,magnanimity, sincerity, earnestness and kindness.
19. A thankful heart is the parent of all virtues. *– A proverb*
20. Vice stings us even in pleasures, but virtue consoles us even in our pain. *– Cotton*
21. God likes him who leads a virtuous life, O Lord, make us virtuous. *– Rigveda*
22. He is ill-clothed that is bare of virtue. *– Benjamin Franklin*
23. No virtue can be great if it is not constant. *– Alfanso Hilagro*
24. Courage is the ladder on which all the other virtues mount. *– Clave Boothe Luce*

Greatness

Greatness stands for nobility and abides in a person's excellence. Greatness has to be earned by our own efforts, for no one is born great. One who dedicates his life to the attainment of noble ideals reaches the threshold of greatness. Name, physique, status or wealth don't make one great. Greatness comes from good qualities like liberality, kindness, holiness, and sensibility. Nobility of character is greatness. A desire for the welfare of the whole humanity and readiness to put it into practice are the symptoms of greatness. Gentle behaviour with all and freedom from egoism reflect greatness.

True greatness comes from the purity of heart and is not subject to praises showered on you. We have not yet seen a great man who is not virtuous. A man of good qualities needs no eulogies. Greatness is always modest and dislikes ostentation. It is meanness to brag about your uprightness. Greatness has a noble attitude towards life. To be great is good but to be good is greater. A great man has no enemies; he has subdued them with love and not with force.

A thinker says: One who has vanquished his enemies is great, but one who has won their love, affection and goodwill is the greatest. It is not worthwhile to overthrow your enemy in a battle but the one who pardons him and wins over him with affection is a true warrior.

The supremacy achieved in a battle-field is not long-lasting. Those who have won the hearts of people are real victors. One who has conquered his own self sets his foot on the road to greatness. The great men whose names occur on the pages of history have been pushed into oblivion because the greatness they attained was false, a meaningless mask. War valiants like Alexander and Akbar were called great, but their greatness was achieved on the point of the sword. On the other hand Asoka who preached the sermon of non-violence on the battle-field penetrated deeper into the heart to give the message of peace and kindness will be remembered for ages.

Great men do not necessarily change the world; they mould themselves, they modify their point of view and when they do so everything appears transformed to them. The people who march against the stream of time have the power to change the world and it is why no great man ever had an easy and comfortable life, he wore a crown of thorns but ruled the heart of the common man. Everything that a great man does is unique. When faced with the smallest trouble of others he forgets his colossal pain and suffering. Rama forgot the pang of separation from Sita when he came upon the wounded Jatayu. Krishna's eyes brimmed with tears when he saw the miserable condition of Sudama. Mahavira was bitten several times when he tried to revive and awaken the serpent, Chand Kaushika, but in return he showered on him the nectar of non-violence, love and compassion. Those who return flowers for thorns, blessings for curses and light for darkness move ahead on the royal road to greatness. Those who remain unmoved by their own sufferings but melt like snow to see others in misery attain immortality. The one who leaves behind him a tale of his nobility is a true great man and his name is recorded in every book of history, religion and culture.

What Others Say

1. The first virtue of all really great men is that they are sincere. *– Anatole France*
2. Great and good are seldom the same man. *– Thomas Fuller*

3. A really great man is known by three signs. Generosity in the design, humanity in the execution, moderation in success. *– Bismarck*

4. To be simple is to be great. *– R.W. Emerson*

5. If any man seeks for greatness, let him forget greatness and ask for truth and he will find both. *– Horace*

6. No great man lives in vain. The history of the world is but the biography of great men. *– Carlyle*

7. The greatest truths are the simplest and so are the great men. *– A.W. Hare*

8. The heights by great men reached and kept, were not attained by sudden flight. But they while their companions slept were toiling upward in the night. *– Longfellow*

9. Lives of great men all remind us;
we can make our lives sublime.
And departing, leave behind us,
foot prints on the sands of time. *– Longfellow*

10. Greatness comes from vision, the tolerance of the spirit, compassion and an even temper which is not ruffled by ill fortune or good fortune. *– Jawaharlal Nehru*

11. A great man is always willing to be little. *– R.W. Emerson*

12. The great man is he who does not lose his child's heart. *– Mencius*

13. Be not afraid of greatness. Some are born great, some achieve greatness, and some have greatness thrust upon them. *– Shakespeare*

Character

Man's character is formed by the way he manages his life. If he leads a planned life and balances his thoughts, speech and conduct even with his smallest habits, he will develop a well-organized personality which will reflect in his character. Conduct of a man plays the most important role in balancing his personality and forms his character which is so important in life. It comprises all the good qualities a man has.

The nature and conduct of a man of good character differ from those of a bad character as much as light differs from darkness. If we are ill-mannered we are on the side of darkness and if we are well-mannered we are on the side of light. Broadly speaking, the little things we do, make up our character which expresses itself through manners. It is our determination to stand firmly and to stick to our resolution in the midst of ups and downs that take place in the world of feelings. A well-mannered person has to pass many tests. The norm of his conduct is that he looks upon other's wife as a mother, scorns others' wealth and is moved by others' pain and suffering as much as by his own. Such a person is truly enlightened. He sets an ideal to be strived for. The root cause of the present decline of our character is the lack of eloquent and vigorous ideals of life. If a person has noble ideals to emulate he will never stumble on the path of life.

Effeminate ideals that overshadow our market and society lead us to immorality which intervenes in our religious life and consequently makes our whole conduct pass through its flames. Now man should rise to the occasion and resolve to oppose its flow. Only animals follow the beaten path. A man of conscience courageously chooses his path and is justly called a man of character, a well-mannered person. And for this one needs no training but determination to develop the technique of regulating himself.

Self-control is the test of our character. If we firmly stick to our resolution in face of the storm of passion, disorder and profligacy raging all round us we plant the seed of the sturdy tree of character. Today a man is adept in making promises but feels no commitment to fulfil them. Of what use are these promises then?

The persons who lack the strength of character commit the crime of breaking their promises. A man is advised to be simple, natural and flexible but this does not apply to his character. A man should behave gently and tenderly with others but he must be very exacting in case of his character and conduct, he must be very strict and strong-willed like a rock. It's only the strength of character that makes a man human.

What Others Say

1. Character is a strange blending of flinty strength and pliable warmth. ***- Robert Shaffer***
2. Character may be manifested in the great moments, but it is made in the small ones. ***– Phillips Brooks***
3. Nearly all men can stand adversity, but if you want to test a man's character, give him power. ***– Abraham Lincoln***
4. Character is what you know you are, not what others think you are. ***– Marva Collins***
5. Character – the willingness to accept responsibility for one's own life is the source from which self-respect springs. ***– Joan Didion***
6. In matters of style, swim with the current, in matters of principle, stand like a rock. ***– Thomas Jefferson***

7. Talents are best nurtured in solitude; character is best formed in the stormy billows of the world. *– Johann Goethe*
8. If I take care of my character, my reputation will take care of itself. *– Dwight L. Moody*
9. A man has no more character than he can command in a time of crisis. *– Ralph W. Sockmann*
10. Good character is not given to us. We have to build it piece by piece – by thought, choice, courage and determination. *– John Luther*
11. Character building the task of life time demands the richest spiritual materials faith, courage, humility, integrity, magnanimity, nobility and abnegation. *– Arenkille Kleiser*
12. All your scholarship would be in vain; if at the same time you do not build your character and attain mastery over your thoughts and actions. *– Mahatma Gandhi*
13. Not education, but character, is man's greatest need, man's greatest safeguard. *– Prophet Mahomet*
14. Wealth, influence, position, power – these are of little value without character. Grandeur of character is moral principle in practice. *– Grenville Kleiser*
15. Truthfulness is a corner-stone of character and if it is not firmly laid in youth, there will ever after be a weak spot in the foundation. *– Jackson Davis.*
16. The crown and glory of life is character. It is the noblest possession of man. It exercises a greater power than wealth and secures all the honour without the jealousies of fame. *– Samuel Smiles.*
17. The greatest hope of society is individual character. *– Canning*
18. Character is destiny. *– Novalis*
19. A man reveals his character even in the simplest thing he does. *– Jean de la Bruyere*
20. Talent will get you to the top, but it takes character to keep you there. *– John Wooden*

Ability

Man's capacity to do a thing is called his ability. Everyone comes here with a unique talent to do something, and when that talent is translated into action it becomes ability. Generally speaking, the specialities required of a man to achieve a purpose are called abilities. We require different abilities to do different things. A blend of knowledge, talent and competence makes an ability. To be able to concentrate on devotion a person needs belief, faith and reverence. To maintain account books of a business enterprise knowledge of arithmetic is essential. Just ability is not enough; it must be used when opportunity calls for it. If it cannot be put into practical use it is meaningless, hence it must be reinforced with intelligence and reasoning.

We need ability in every field of life as much as we need it to lead our life and discharge our responsibilities to our family, society and nation. Ability is both innate and acquired. In Gita, Sri Krishna says that adeptness to do a work is called Yoga. Your ability is measured by the skill with which you do a thing. Work becomes easy and reaches a successful conclusion if it is done by a skilled person. On the other hand, if done by an unskilled novice it gets garbled and is unsuccessful. Ability sharpens our competence and enables us to do the most complicated work in a way that quality-wise it is judged best. If an unskilled person attempts the same thing he makes a number of mistakes and spoils it. Faultless performance of work is in no way less than worship and it has been rightly said that work is worship. The society and the government should devise a system of education that imparts required insight and efficiency to every citizen of the country.

Instead of producing highly finished and competent citizens our schools today have become a factory churning out clerks. Vocational education must be supplemented by academic and cultural education for only conscientious and dutiful citizens can be expected to have good ideas and be cultured. The teachers should come forward and assist the parents in inculcating in children good manners right from the childhood, to create a healthy and clean social atmosphere. The children of today are the citizens of tomorrow; hence their skill, talent and competence should be refined and polished.

Religious institutions as well as saints and seers should make active efforts for the training of the youth. They should earnestly devote themselves to the task of popularizing meditation and yogic exercises to improve the mental health and Yoga should be propagated as a form of worshipping. It gives mental peace, develops competence and refines ability.

All parents, teachers both secular and religious, society and the government should make concerted efforts to train able citizens to give a new direction to the country. What we need is collective effort, for well-qualified, faithful, loyal and dutiful citizens may be prepared with cooperative effort alone. It is these who will lay the foundation of a strong and successful nation.

What Others Say

1. As we advance in life, we learn the limits of our abilities.
   – ***Fronse***

2. Ability is of little account without opportunity. – ***Napoleon***

3. Everyone excels in something in which another fails.
   – ***Latin Proverb***

4. We judge ourselves by what we feel capable of doing, while others judge us by what we have already done. – ***H.W. Longfellow***

5. Ability is what you're capable of doing. – ***Lou Holtz***

6. Ability will never catch up with the demand for it. – ***Malcolm S. Forbes***

7. Discipline is the refining fire by which talent becomes ability. – ***Roy L. Smith***

8. Intelligence is quickness to apprehend as distinct from ability, which is capacity to act wisely on the thing apprehended. – ***A.N. Whitehead***

Manliness

Our ancient sages have prescribed four goals of man's life – dharma (righteousness), artha (money), kama (desire) and moksha (salvation). The first goal i.e. righteousness lays the foundation of man's progress and advancement in life. Explaining this concept, the acharyas have said that it helps in the physical, moral and spiritual development of our life. Next comes money or wealth regarding which there are two points of view. One that money is essential to meet our material requirements. It is essential to a householder's life as it helps in maintaining social relations with other people Defining money acharya Somadeva says that money is the means of realizing all the other goals of life. In its absence they all appear meaningless. So money enjoys the same place in the material world as righteousness enjoys in the spiritual world.

The second point of view holds that although money is important in life, it is not everything. Only, the money earned through upright means is meaningful and useful. It must be acquired through just, ethical and socially approved channels. It is placed after righteousness so that it may be sanctified by uprightness. Money earned by unethical and unjust means is fruitless and mischievous; it drags us to evil ways.

Placing desire after money signifies that we should entertain desires only when we have earned money enough to meet them. Desire stands for sense gratification, for all senses crave indulgence and pleasure which comes from consumption of various things. This sense gratification is classed as passion. Our desires remain unfulfilled in the absence of money but the acharyas recommend that money should be regulated by righteousness and desires must adapt both to righteousness and wealth.

Salvation is the final goal of manliness. It is the highest goal, the culmination of all the others which gain meaning only when they lead to it. An acharya has gone to the extent of saying that the righteousness, wealth and desire that lead to salvation are not mutually contradictory and rather they cooperate with each other and do not remain despicable when regulated by righteousness.

Duty

To live in society we need both rights and duties. Rights always imply certain duties associated with them and thus they complement each other.

Generally speaking, duty means what we are expected to do. We have to do something for ourselves and something for our family, society, nation and the world. These are our duties. There are certain obligations and duties which all of us must discharge to elude punishment. Even if we are acquitted by a court of law our case remains pending in the court of the Lord. Remember, you can demand your rights only when you are willing to perform your duties.

Our first duty is to acquire knowledge about ourselves and to ever remain conscious that we have an inner–self. The best thing for man is to do his duty and leave the rest to God.

What is one man's right is other man's duty. If everyone conscientiously discharges his duty everyone else will automatically get his rights.

Now let us cast a glance at our present day life style. We indulge in what we should not do and neglect what we should. This creates a mischievous situation. When we take to unpropitious activities we try to eschew our duty and it infects our mind. Indian metaphysics holds that mind controls our actions which in their turn affect our mind. Our participation in some illicit activities infects our thoughts and ideas which in turn influence our conduct. Thus the violation of our duty vitiates our whole life.

The most deplorable aspect of the consumer culture is that it has made man oblivious of his duty and he raises slogans only to demand his rights. The man negligent about his duty is not justified in asking his rights.

An important question arises here. How can we decide what is and what is not our duty? We can answer it in a nutshell. Do a hundred good turns to a man and ask him to reciprocate only one. But today things have reversed; we do one duty and demand a hundred rights. Our seers say that one right is equal to a hundred duties. We come across innumerable examples in society where people are fully enjoying their rights but totally neglecting their duties.

Here is a moral tale. A gardener and a potter who were intimate friends purchased a camel and two large pannier bags to carry on a joint business. They hitched the bags on the camel's back so that the gardener could load his vegetables on one side and the potter his pitchers on the other. One day while they were going to the market with their camel, the gardener got tired and lagged behind. The potter followed the camel who now turned its neck and began to browse vegetables. The potter condoned it thinking it would not harm him. Soon the camel finished all the vegetables, the pannier bags lost balance and the one with pitchers fell on the ground with a thud. The potter now realized that he suffered this heavy loss for he had neglected his duty of safeguarding other's rights. This tale clearly points out the inter-dependence of rights and duties.

What Others Say

1. Make it a point to do something every day that you don't want to do. This is the golden rule for acquiring the habit of doing your duty without pain. – ***Mark Twain***
2. The path of duty is the way to glory. – ***Tennyson***

3. Truth is a divine word. Duty is divine law.
– D.C. Mackintosh

4. One's own duty though appears to be mundane, is preferable to the duty of another, well-performed. Even death in the performance of one's own duty brings blessedness, another's duty is fraught with danger of downfall. *– Bhagavad Gita*

5. Duty is a very personal thing. It is what comes from knowing the need to take action and not, just a need to urge others to do something. *– Mother Teresa*

6. Every duty is holy and devotion to duty is the highest form of worship of God. *– Swami Vivekananda*

7. Never mind your happiness; do your duty. *– Will Durant*

8. Duty before pleasure.

9. Duty determines destiny.

10. God never imposes a duty without giving the time to perform it.

Speech

Speech for a humanbeing is a bridge that links his thoughts and ideas with the visible world. It helps him in developing and expanding his talent. Animals are also endowed with speech but they cannot use it meaningfully. With man, speech is a great property which enables him to expand his acquaintance and express experiences of his cogitation and reflection. Thoughts and experiences expressed in words by our saints and seers are now remembered as golden words, maxims and moral truths. Speech that is meaningless and serves no purpose is called babbling or prattling because speech by definition implies meaningful use of words to express feelings and ideas.

The words we use should be well-chosen and express truth. If besides being truthful they are useful also men of understanding would make them part of their life and conduct. Today people say pleasant things just to flatter others and unearth their secrets. And in the name of telling the truth cause them pain or create trouble. People will not appreciate your speech unless it is both truthful and pleasant. You will be ridiculed if what you say is only pleasing flattery without a grain of truth in it.

History is full of instances which show that an imprudent and heedless use of words has led to a number of battles. Mahabharat tells us that Draupadi jokingly and unwillingly addressed the Kauravas as blind for being the offspring of the blind king Dhritrashtra and caused the flagrant decimation of the armies of both the Pandavas and the Kauravas. Even today in every household there are instances of bickerings and quarrels caused by unrestrained use of words. In this difficult plight a man should learn how to use words that suit the occasion. He should also be economical in their use because superfluous words often create unpleasantness. Frugality of words is a kind of silence and makes your speech pregnant with sagacity. It is why all religious thinkers have praised silence calling it the language of soul. In the silent moments of prayer soul establishes contact with the Lord. We should make silence and economy of words a habit and part of our life and character. Moreover, silence is a perennial source of energy.

A thinker says: Restrain speech if you can; avoid speech if you can do with signs and don't shout if you can get things done with soft voice. One who follows this injunction attains dignity of speech. It is an art and those who practise it are called wizards of speech. Their words go straight to the heart, win over people and leave an indelible impress on them.

What Others Say

1. Speech is civilization itself. The word, even the most contradictory word, preserves contact – it is silence which isolates. – ***Thomas Mann***

2. Darts, barbed arrow, iron-headed spears, however deep they penetrate the flesh, may be extracted, but a cutting speech that pierces like a javelin to the heart, none can remove; it lies and rankles there. – ***Mahabharat***

3. Nature has given man one tongue and two ears, that we may hear twice as much as we speak. – ***Epictetus***

4. A superior man is modest in his speech, but exceeds in his actions. – ***Confucius***

5. A wise man reflects before he speaks, a fool speaks and then reflects on what he has uttered. – ***A French Proverb***

6. Men of few words are the best men. – ***Shakespeare***

7. Hear much, speak little. – ***Bias***

8. Speaking without thinking is shooting without taking aim. *– Ancient Proverb*

9. Let your speech be always with grace, seasoned with salt. *– Colossians*

10. A soft answer turneth away wrath. *– Proverbs*

11. Teach your child to hold his tongue; he'll learn fast enough to speak.

12. Much speaking and lying are cousins.

13. Speech is a mirror of the soul as a man speaks so he is. *– Publilius Syrus*

14. Speak but little and well if you would be esteemed a man of merit. *– Trench*

15. Discretion of speech is more than eloquence. *– Francis Bacon*

16. You can suffocate a thought by expressing it with too many words. *– Frank A. Clark*

17. The most valuable of all talents is that of never using two words when one will do. *– Thomas Jefferson*

18. The genius of communication is the ability to be both totally honest and totally kind at the same time. *– John Powell*

19. Use soft words and hard arguments. *– English Proverb*

Humility

The lesson on humility is the first that we are taught in the school of Nature. The trees bow down, the creepers hang low, flowers gently and cheerfully spread their fragrance. Water rises high when it flows down and its rise is proportionate to the height from which it falls. You may be endowed with several great qualities but politeness is the crown of humility. Humility means that you bow as the fruit laden branches bow towards the earth. They very well know that it is all because of mother earth's grace that they got all the fruit. Similarly, man owes all his wealth to God's grace and this fills him with a sense of humility smashing the false presumption that he is the doer.

Humility enhances the attributes of a person hence he should never feel proud of his wealth, beauty, power or knowledge. 'He must really be taller than you if he has to bow to greet you,' is a golden saying. The big should conduct themselves as small because the one who thinks that he is big is really small whereas the one who behaves as a small person attains a higher status.

Encounter with difficulties and shocks makes a man wise and humble. Egoism is very dangerous because it often appears in the guise of humility, therefore a really wise man is advised to be humble. Your humility ought to be condemned if you are vain of it. If you wish to attain knowledge, be humble and when you have attained it be humbler because fruit laden trees bend down to earth. The water laden clouds hang low. The same is the case with gentlemen who have acquired wealth and are philanthropic by nature. They are always meek and unassuming. A thinker says, 'I practised humility and received love and respect from one and all.'

Humility disarms all rivalry. The root of our suffering and struggle is egoism. The one who has broken free of this prison house and adopted humility as a trait of life can cheerfully face any trouble in life. Guru Nanak has rightly said:

Remain as low as the grass, says Nanak
Overgrown grass burns while
The low remains green.

Corroborating the same idea Bihari says:

Man and water behave the same way
The steep they flow, the higher they rise.

The nature of man and water is the same. The slope of the fall determines the height they can rise to.

A seer is of the view that the world wants to uplift the person who bends low but uproots the one who is arrogant and ostentatious. A river in flood carries away the tall large trees standing on its bank but leaves the soft and tender grass and straws unharmed by its fierce splashes. All our scriptures unanimously testify that every saint, seer or hermit has insisted on the attainment of humility as the first stage in the spiritual journey. If you are not humble it is impossible for you to acquire wisdom. It has rightly been said:

We have learnt neither by smiling nor by crying,
Whatever we have learnt is from submission
to someone.

A simple, unaffected and humble person turns even poison into nectar whereas the arrogant turns even the nectar into opium. Adopt humility in life and see how the world embraces you and raises you to great heights.

What Others Say

1. The tree laden with fruits always bends low. If you wish to be great, be lowly and meek. – ***Sri Ramakrishna***

2. I believe the first test of a truly great man is his humility. – ***John Ruskin***

3. Basically, humility is the attitude of one who stands constantly under the judgement of God. It is the attitude of one who is like the soul. – ***Antony Bloom***

4. The hour of the greatest triumph is the hour of the greatest humility. – ***Mahatma Gandhi***

5. We come nearest to the great when we are great in humility. – ***R.N. Tagore***

6. Pride changed angels into devils; humility makes man into angels. – ***St. Augustine.***

7. Pride ends in destruction, humility ends in honour. – ***Bible***

8. To be humble to the superiors is duty, to equals courtesy to inferiors nobleness. – ***Benjamin Franklin***

9. Humility is the root, mother, nurse, foundation and bond of all virtues. – ***Chrysostom***

10. The only cure for vanity is laughter. And the only fault that is laughable is vanity. – ***Henri Bergson***

Self-respect

Self-respect makes our life worthwhile and its absence insignificant. Egoism differs from self-respect as much as poison differs from nectar. Arrogance is a vice while self-respect is a virtue. The simplest definition of self-respect is: Make efforts to lead a dignified life and achieve dignity by cultivating virtues. One who is careful about the values of life enjoys true self-respect. It means that he is awake and conscious about his existence.

Everyone must have self-respect. We must be proud of our country, our nation, our character, our culture and our civilization. Self-respect is born of our personality when it has certain essential and inalienable qualities. We must have a will to defend our self-respect in all circumstances.

Self-respect gives birth to certain qualities of personality which generate self-confidence in life. It is forbearance to condone someone's undesirable or villainous behaviour but we should never brook an attack on our self-respect; we must promptly rise to defend it at any cost. We should refuse the greatest advantage if it strikes our self-respect. Rahim exhorts us:

Stay, O Rahim, till you get gifts and warm welcome.
When they are missing, promptly bid adieu to that place.

You should stay at a place as long as people offer you warm welcome and honourable reception and entertain you lovingly and joyfully, but as soon as you feel that they are hurting your self-respect by their indifference or neglect, you should immediately quit that place.

Arrogance and vanity are beastly qualities, self-respect is an attribute of humanity, but the absence of all the three confers divinity on you. Arrogance is opposed to self-respect as the night is opposed to day. Arrogance pushes us into the ditch of degradation and decline whereas self-respect lifts us to great triumph. In fact a man of self-respect is sincerely committed to high human values and this makes him morally scrupulous. To hurt his self-respect means that you doubt his principles. A person feels enraged and hisses like a serpent when some one hurts his self-respect or casts a slur on it. He may possess serenity, depth and tranquility of a sea but when his self-respect is challenged his mind is ruffled by tsunami waves.

To move out of the darkness of egoism into the sunshine of self-respect means that you have broken the bonds of snobbery and self-centredness, for the life of a man of self-respect is simple, gentle and sweet. His head is always bent low with humility whereas an egotist always behaves ostentatiously. The stiffness of egotism makes a man dead though still moving and breathing, whereas a man of self-respect is always lively and cheerful. He not only protects his self-respect but also esteems that of others.

A man of self-respect is sensitive by nature and knows its value whereas an arrogant person is intolerant. He is cautious about his vanity but is always on the look out to disgrace and humiliate others. Come out of the prison house of egotism and move on the golden road of self-respect. This will elevate and glorify your life.

What Others Say

1. Morale is self-respect in action. – ***Avery Weisman***
2. Lack of something to feel important about is almost the greatest tragedy a man may have. – ***Arthur E. Morgan***

3. Self-respect is the fruit of discipline; the sense of dignity grows with the ability to say no to oneself.
   – ***Abraham Joshua Heschel***

4. Trust yourself. You know more than you think you do.
   – ***Benjamin Spock***

5. Self-respect is the corner stone of all virtue.
   – ***Sir John Herschel***

6. Self-respect the secure feeling that no one, as yet, is suspicious. – ***H. L. Mencken***

7. For a self-respecting man infame is worse than death.
   – ***Anonymous***

8. He that respects himself is safe from others; he wears a coat of mail that none can pierce. – ***Henry W. Longfellow***

Truth

To take a thing, an idea or a way of living as it is in reality is called truth. It is not possible to define truth in words. It surrounds our life like light. It is endless, unfashionable and imperishable and whatever part of it we are able to grasp or realize becomes the truth of our life. What is present and real is true. Truth is a way of life as well as a philosophy. It does not conceal anything nor can it be concealed. It comes out sooner or later as the sun appears out of the clouds.

Truth is multidimensional but we can see only one aspect of it at a time, hence sometimes there arises a doubt about it. Infact, truth is non-contradictory but sometimes it speaks in paradoxes and appears mysterious like God. Truth finds an expression in our speech as well as in our conduct and behaviour.

One great advantage of speaking the truth is that you need not remember what you told a particular person. If you wish people to behave truthfully with you try to be truthful yourself. This will leave a favourable impression on others. The journey of truth may be difficult and prickly but its destination is tender and fragrant like flowers. You are, therefore, advised never to deviate from the path of truth however difficult it might be; never resort to lie though it might serve your immediate purpose.

Truth is a great thing in itself and it would be better if truth prevails and falsehood disappears. Truth takes birth in ideas and finds expression in speech and behaviour. One who lives the truth needs perform no worship or religious rites and rituals for truth is righteousness incarnate. As soon as we assimilate it all evil disappears from life.

The wise men distinguish two forms of truth: transcendental truth and practical truth. When transcendental truth dawns on us the whole world appears an illusion but practical truth guides us on the path of life. Hence our way of life should combine both of them. There are people who create an illusion of truth also. Truth is straightforward, simple and natural and shines like the sun whereas to tell a lie we have to exert much and concoct many excuses.

Unfortunately some people live under the misapprehension that at present only the lie prevails and truth has no use. But this is just an excuse invented by liars to cloak their own falsehood. In fact, man lives by truth and not by falsehood. Just cast a glance at your daily routine and you will find that out of twenty-four hours you speak the truth for twenty-three hours and a half and use a lie only for less than half an hour. Then why do you feel that you cannot lead your life on the strength of truth?

Our seers say that if you use a lie even for a moment it infringes your truthful conduct and righteous behaviour for the whole day. You cannot turn a pitcher of poison into nectar by pouring a little bowl of nectar into it, but even a single drop of poison into the pitcher of nectar turns it into poison. Take care that not even a drop of poison falls into the pitcher of your life. The life of those who speak the truth is clean and transparent. And if you wish to have a clean healthy lifestyle follow the truth and through this welcome gate let greatness enter your life. Then your life will become an ideal life and serve as a beacon light for the whole world.

What Others Say

1. Great is truth and mighty above all things. *– Bible*

2. The aim of the superior man is truth. *– Confucius*

3. We swallow greedily any lie that flatters us, but we sip only little by little at a truth we find bitter. *– Danis Diderot*

4. Truth is tough. *– Oliver Wendell Holmes*

5. Truth is often eclipsed but never extinguished. *– Livy*

6. A great truth is a truth whose opposite is also a truth. *– Thomas Mann*

7. The love of truth has its reward in heaven and even on earth. *– Friedrich Nietzche*

8. Truth is no road to fortune. *– Rousseau*

9. Life is short, but truth works for and lives long; let us speak the truth. *– Arthur Shopenhauer*

10. Truth is the only safe ground to stand upon. *– Elizabeth Cady Stanton*

11. Truth is on the march, nothing can stop it now. *– Emile Zola*

12. Art is truth, and truth is religion. *– Thackerey*

13. Truth leads to righteousness and righteousness to heaven. *– Hadis*

14. God can be realized by having truth in the heart. *– Manduka*

15. Truth stands the test of time, lies are soon exposed. *– Bible*

16. The language of truth is unadorned and always simple. *– Marcellinus Ammianus*

17. Speaking truth is like writing fair, and only comes by practice. *– John Ruskin*

18. Craft must have clothes, but truth loves to go naked. *– Thomas Fuller*

19. He is true in the truest sense of the word who is true in thought, word and deed. *– Koran*

20. Truth can be sweet or bitter, but it can never be bad. A lie can be sweet or bitter, but it can never be good. *– Constance Virgil*

21. Truth always originates in a minority of one, and every custom begins as a broken precedent. *– Will Durant*

Non-violence II

Non-violence is man's innate nature, but violence his creation. Man is not beastly by nature, but an animal is. Man has passed through that stage but still retains traces of its experience. In fact, humanity begins by choice and man lives by determination, by resolution. Man often faces a dilemma but an animal never. All animals follow a predictable path, they have no choice. Violence can be discarded and non-violence adopted. And once non-violence is accepted, it is difficult to discard. Man may be violent but he can relinquish it, for it is not his true nature.

There are a number of misconceptions about non-violence. Some think that the earth belongs to man, he is its sole master and other creatures have no right to live and thrive here. The ideology prevails on him to kill or have wild animals such as monkeys, deer and others killed, or he may tacitly approve killing them. It is simply another way of justifying that might is right. This egocentricity reveals our wild nature devoid of any trace of modesty or fairness. Who has leased this earth to man? In fact, every creature born on this earth has equal right to live and draw sustenance from it. Man cannot deprive others of their right simply because he is more powerful than they. If he does so, he is sure to be punished by nature.

Generally, non-violence makes you quiver with sympathy for others' suffering. In other words, a sight of pain or sorrow of someone whether related or unrelated melts us without any bias to his caste or religion, province or nation. Or simply a mention of someone's distress prompts you to relieve him of it. The benevolent say that non-violence moves your heart at one's discomfort and sows the seed of charity there. So says the Gunbhushan Shrawakachar.

All creatures crave long life, desire joy and happiness and shun pain and suffering. Affection and sympathy for all living creatures and a sense of unity with them means compassion. There is a fine dividing live between kindness, pity and compassion. Kindness implies sympathy for others and prompts us to action. If you are shocked at someone's wretchedness, you feel pity. But if you feel a conscious kinship and an inclination to help, it is compassion. In it a man first analyses his own feelings to find out what are his interests or in what lies his happiness. Then he establishes an affinity with the feelings of others. Thus compassion has a spiritual content which makes him feel one with the others and empathize with them.

What Others Say

1. The kingdom of Heaven is Ahimsa.
2. Non-violence is not a cover for cowardice but it is the supreme virtue of the brave.
3. There is no such thing as defeat or despair in the dictionary of a man who bases his life on truth and ahimsa. – ***Mahatma Gandhi***
4. Whosoever shall smite thee on thy right cheek, turn to him the other also. – ***Bible***
5. Non-violence is the first article of my faith. It is also the last article of my creed.

Inspirational Quotes

1. To act alone you have the right, never for its fruits. Let not the longing for fruits be the motive force of your action. At the same time, let not this stipulation lead you to persist in indolent inaction. ***– Bhagvad Gita***
2. Advice is seldom welcome; and those who need it most, always like it the least. ***– Chesterfield***
3. There is no education like adversity. ***– Disraeli***
4. The world makes way for a man who knows where he is going. ***– Dryden***
5. The bird wishes it were a cloud.
The cloud wishes it were a bird. ***– Rabindranath Tagore***
6. A good book is the precious life blood of a master spirit, embalmed and treasured up on purpose to a life beyond. ***– Milton***
7. The courage we desire and prize is not the courage to die decently, but to live manfully. ***– Carlyle***
8. The greatest test of courage on earth is to bear defeat without losing heart. ***– Ingersoll***
9. Nations like individuals, live and die; but civilization survives. ***– Mazzini***
10. Avoid the man of temper, the selfish, the boastful, the scornful, the liar, lest you acquire his ways of thinking. ***–Anonymous***
11. The human mind is attracted to growth, beginning and freshness. Compassion thus is the force of growth and development while anger is destruction. ***– Dalai Lama***

12. Confession is the first step to repentance. – *Edmund Gayton*
13. Be courteous to all, but intimate with few; and let those few be well tried before you give them your confidence. –*Washington*
14. Conscience is God's presence in man. – *Swedenberg*
15. Sweet are the thoughts that savour of content. The quiet mind is richer than a crown. – *R. Greene*
16. Culture is 'to know the best that has been said and thought in the world'. – *Mathew Arnold*
17. We are not here to curse the darkness, but to light the candle that can guide us through the darkness to a safe and sane future. – *John Kennedy*
18. Death is certain for the born and rebirth inevitable for the dead. You should not grieve over the inevitable. – *Bhagavad Gita*
19. He who is always the friend of all, and who through thought, word and deed, is absorbed in promoting the welfare of all, knows what is dharma. – *Mahabharat*
20. Difficulty is a severe instructor. – *Burke*
21. Each soul is potentially divine. The goal is to manifest this divinity within by controlling nature, external and internal. – *Swami Vivekananda*
22. Acquire knowledge. It enables the possessers to distinguish the right from the wrong; it lightens up the path to Heaven. It is a friend in the desert, our company is solitude, our companion when friendless. It guides to happiness, it sustains in adversity. It is an ornament among friends and an armour against enemies. – *Koran*
23. The wise man learns more from his enemies than the fool from his friends. – *Jacques Deval*
24. Enthusiasm leads to success. Euthusiasm is happiness. Enthusiasm is always the driving force to all actions. – *The Ramayana*

25. A man can make mistakes, but only an idiot persists in his error. *– Cicero*
26. Real failure comes only when we forget our ideals, objectives and principles and begin to wander away from the road which leads to their realization. *–Jawaharlal Nehru*
27. Fame is the perfume of heroic deeds *– Socrates*
28. Fate bows to the man who defies it. *– Swami Ramtirth*
29. Fear always springs from ignorance. *– Emerson*
30. Fortune and love befriend the bold. *– Ovid*
31. Genius means a transcendent capacity for taking trouble. *– Carlyle*
32. Great minds have purposes, others have wishes. *– Washington Irving*
33. There is this difference between happiness and wisdom; he that thinks himself the happiest man is really so; but he that thinks himself the wisest man is generally the greatest fool. *– Colton*
34. The most happy is he who most promotes the happiness of others. *– Zarathustra*
35. When you are good to others, you are best to yourself. *– Dale Carnegie*
36. Everybody thinks of changing humanity but nobody thinks of changing oneself. *– Leo Tolstoy*
37. Everything has beauty, but not every one sees it. *– Confucius*
38. A smile is the light in your window that tells others that there is a caring, sharing person inside. *– Denis Waitley*
39. If there were in the world today any large number of people who desired their own happiness more than they desired the unhappiness of others, we could have paradise in a few years. *– Bertrand Russell*

40. Three passions have governed my life. The longings for love, the search for knowledge and unbearable pity for the suffering of human kind. – ***Bertrand Russell***
41. Do hundreds of small but good deeds, everyday. One fine day one would become very big.
42. The essence of education lies in drawing out the very best that is in you.
43. It is the mark of the cultured man that he is aware of the fact that equality is an ethical and not a biological principle.
44. Imagination and fiction make up more than three quarters of our real life.
45. Forget the harm that the others have done to you, and forget the goods that you have done to others.
46. Chances happen to all, but to turn chances to account is the gift of a few.
47. As a general rule the most successful man in life is the man who has the best information.
48. Nature often holds up a mirror so we can see more clearly the ongoing processes of growth, renewal, and transformation in our lives. – ***Mary Aun Brussat***
49. Method is more important than strength. By dropping golden beads near a snake, a crow once managed to have a passer-by kill the snake for the beads. – ***Siddha Nagarjuna***
50. A teacher affects eternity; he can never tell where his influence stops. – ***H. B. Adams***

Pity

Pity is a tender feeling that enables a man to experience at his emotional level the pain of others. When the tale of pain and suffering moves a person, the spring of pity gushes out in his heart. Pity does not mean that you yourself live in pain and misery but indicates that you make an effort to drive away the pain and suffering of others. Sensitiveness, sympathy, kindness and pity – all are closely related feelings. A man is known by these qualities. Pity and compassion are the qualities we beget in the company of gentle people, or by reading good books or thinking and acting on good thoughts.

When the feeling of compassion arises in a man he sees himself in others and others in himself. Compassion is the divine light of our inner self that enables us to see the reflection of God. Small acts of kindness, a few words of love convert our earth into a paradise but when the angel of kindness is driven out of our heart man becomes crusty and turns into a serpent slithering in a desert.

Let God be the judge, man must treat others kindly. Everyone expects that others take pity on him but when it is his own turn he shirks from it. Those who are not kind to the poor will be tortured by the mighty and muscular.

In the light of these remarks, now try to recall if you have ever felt the stream of compassion flowing inside you. Have you ever wiped tears from some one's eyes even in a dream? If yes, a divine spirit abides in you in human form. That divine spirit kind to everyone is an epitome of compassion. If you entertain feelings of compassion your heart and ideas become divine and make you generous to others. No doubt your own suffering sears you, but when others' suffering suffuses your eyes and melts your heart it means that divine feelings are rising in you.

The divine personalities who try to find out means of relieving others of their pain and suffering without caring for their own are remembered even after centuries. Rama was desperately distressed when Sita was kidnapped but the sight of the wounded Jatayu made him forget all about it. When Sri Krishna saw poverty-stricken Sudama at his gate he was carried away by pity and hailed him with suffused eyes.

Rama and Krishan owe their greatness to this great perennial font of compassion flowing in their heart. With the milk of compassion, Mahavir cured the snake Chandkaushik of its malevolent nature and Buddha performed the same miracle with Augulimal. These eminent persons were compassion incarnate and instead of cursing the sin requited ambrosia for virulence and dispelled darkness from their lives. It is why they are remembered even today. We remember those who live for others and burn like incense to give off fragrance.

The world torn by acrimony and discord needs a shower of compassion which has become all the more important because our heart has become desolate as a desert. The whole atmosphere is rent by hatred, rivalry and revenge, light a lamp of kindness and turn it into a heaven.

What Others Say

1. The truly brave are soft of heart and eyes, and feel for what their duty bids them do. *– Byron*
2. He that pities another remembers himself. *– George Herbert*
3. Pity is a perception of our own misfortune in those of others. *– La Rochefoucauld*

4. The quality of mercy is not strained. It droppeth as the gentle rain from heaven. *– Shakespeare*

5. No beast so fierce but knows some touch of pity. *– Shakespeare*

6. Blessed are the merciful for they shall obtain mercy. *– Bible*

7. In case of doubt it is best to lean to the side of mercy. *– Legal Maxim*

8. Kindness is the foundation of all religions; pride the parent of all sins. *– Saint Tulsidas*

9. A part of kindness consists in loving people more than they deserve. *– J. Joubert*

10. Kindness gives birth to kindness. *– Sophocles*

11. Little deeds of kindness, little words of love, help to make earth happy like the heaven above. *– Julia A. F. Carney*

12. I expect to pass through this world but once any good thing therefore that I can do, or any kindness that I can show to any fellow creature, let me do it and now let me not defer or neglect it, for I shall not pass this way again. *– Stephen Grellet*

13. Resolve to be tender with the young; compassionate with the aged, sympathetic with the striving, and tolerant with the weak and the wrong. Sometime in life you will have been all of these. *– Bob Goddard*

14. Make no judgments where you have no compassion. *– Anne Mecaffey*

15. If you want others to be happy, practise compassion. If you want to be happy, practise compassion. *– Dalai Lama*

16. A little kindness from person to person is better than a vast love for all human kind. *– Richard Dehmel*

17. Life is short and never have enough time for gladdening the hearts of those who travel the way with us. Oh, be swift to love! Make haste to be kind.

    – Henri Frederic Amiel

18. Kindness consists in loving people more than they deserve. *– Joseph Joubert*

19. Kindness is never wasted. If it has no effect on the recipient, at least it benefits the bestower.

    – S.H. Simmons.

20. A warm smile is the universal language of kindness.

    – William Arthur Ward

Forgiveness

In a civilized society begging forgiveness and forgiving have special importance. It may take place between two individuals closely related to each other or between two groups or two nations. If someone earnestly begs forgiveness and is not disrespectful, he will make you forgiving by nature. It has a curative effect. I have always noticed how in the absence of forgiveness all those who humiliated me for small things or were humiliated by me sulked for the rest of their life under the burden of complaints and criticism. If both had earnestly forgiven each other they would have been spared of this unnecessary mental tension.

In fact, the Hebrew scripture Talmud declares at one place that God created repentance before creating the universe. Perhaps He already knew that man would make a number of mistakes and beg forgiveness in the form of repentance.

In the process of forgiveness there is an exchange of modesty and power between the one who hurt and the one who was hurt. Your behaviour accords power of forgiving to the one who was hurt and you yourself feel modest for your action. Thus an exchange of power and modesty is inherent in forgiving. People wrongly equate forgiving with weakness whereas it requires a great strength of character. If you don't pay in the same coin for something unpleasant or for some offence done by a person it is called forgiving. Someone misbehaved with us and admitted his mistake and we assured him not to retaliate. This assurance is called forgiving. Forgiveness is a synonym of generosity, greatness and modesty. If you forgive someone it does not lower your status nor does it reduce his respect and honour. On the contrary, both grow day after day. Forgiving puts an end to anger and tension and fills the mind with peace and pleasure.

What Others Say

1. To err is human, to forgive, divine. – ***Alexander Pope***
2. When you stand in prayer, forgive whatever you have against anybody. – ***Jesus Christ***
3. The weak cannot forgive, forgiveness is the attribute of the strong. – ***Mahatma Gandhi***
4. Forgiveness is the noblest revenge. – ***Anonymous***
5. Forgive, and ye shall be forgiven. – ***Bible***
6. The more a man knows, the more he forgives. – ***Catherine, the Great***
7. The day the child realizes that all adults are imperfect he becomes an adolescent, the day he forgives them, he becomes an adult; the day he forgives himself he becomes wise. – ***Alden Nowlan***
8. Never does the human soul appear so strong and noble as when it forgives revenge and dares to forgive an enemy. – ***E.H. Chapin***
9. He who cannot forgive others destroys the bridge over which he himself must pass. – ***George Herbert***
10. When a deep injury is done us, we never recover until we forgive. – ***Alan Paton***
11. Forgiveness is a gift of high value. Yet its cost is nothing. – ***Betty Smith***

Service

Service adds fragrance to human life. Without service man's life is like an artificial flower which though beautiful has no fragrance. The life without service is meaningless. It becomes purposeful and profitable when the heart is full of compassion and the body is ready to serve others.

Service is a concrete expression of love and sympathy. To selflessly cooperate with a person in the way he desires or to do what he requires is service. We must plan our daily routine in such a way that we get time to do a good turn. Service is a duty; it earns us merit and is an ornament of humanity. God likes it most. If you serve sincerely, your name will be recorded in the register of the Lord. The name inscribed on stones here is obliterated one day.

Even the most affluent person cannot justify his wealth if he lacks the noble quality of service. There is a saying: If you are rich prepare your body and mind to serve others without expecting anything from them. The weariness of one willing to serve others disappears automatically. Service acts as a bridge between the people.

Service is an accompanying musical instrument for a song of love between two souls. Apart from human beings, God also takes service to humanity as service to Him. It is a puff of wind that transports the individual soul to the Supreme Bliss. It is like a sandalwood wand that leaves its fragrance both in the hand that holds it and that receives it. Service is a divine duty, so perform it heartily without making a display of it. Serving others means that you do something which is both useful and pleasant. It pleases at the moment and proves useful in the long run. It requires no material objects but only a feeling of devotion and sincerity.

This service becomes a prayer if we remember the name of God while performing it. A true devotee of God is always willing to serve the world for service is the ideal of his life. God wishes that instead of sitting idle in a lonely forest and singing hymns in His praise, we should relieve the pain of a suffering human-being and make him happy. God has given us two arms to support and lift those that are sinking. Service is a concrete expression of an ascetic's perfection and he should make it a point to do an act of welfare everyday.

Service does not mean that we organize large scale programmes of public welfare. Instead of serving the common people they often aim at exhibition and publicity. The true service consists in silently presenting a vision of hope before the eyes suffused with tears. We should covertly help the destitute to relieve their poverty and misery. But unfortunately most of the programmes of public service are motivated by a desire for fame and praise. It is not a true and genuine service, for the true service emerges from a sense of dedication and sacrifice. It never expects a return in the long run too.

Under the impact of western culture we have restricted the meaning of service. In fact, it is not just an act of individual welfare or cooperation; it is a philosophy of life. A person while serving the other does not think that he is doing something philanthropic, he feels motivated by a divine urge to do so. He feels obliged that he got an opportunity to carry out the instruction of God. In the core of his heart he feels convinced that he has done something good for himself and not for others. The sympathetic pain that rose in his heart at the sight of a grief-stricken person is amply allayed when he provides relief to him and in a way soothes his own pain. When you are moved by such feelings your life begins to emit a sweet perfume.

What Others Say

1. He who wishes to secure the good of others, has already secured his own. – ***Confucius***
2. There is a direct link between service to others and rewards in life. – ***Arikier***
3. This body is for service to others. – ***Kalidasa***
4. Service can have no meaning unless one takes pleasure in it. When it is done for show or for fear of public opinion, it stunts the man and crushes his spirit. – ***Mahatma Gandhi***
5. The service we render others is really the rent we pay for our room on this earth. – ***Wilfred Grenfell***
6. He profits most who serves best. – ***Arthur F. Sheldon***
7. So long as we love we serve; so long as we are loved we are indispensable. – ***R. L. Stevenson***

Love

The four letters of the word 'Love' contain not only the secret of life but also its duty and action plan. In the absence of love we cannot decide what we should do and how we can sanctify it with righteousness. Love is a strange feeling; it fills our heart with pleasure. It is a puff of scented wind which soothes the inner consciousness and thrills us with joy. The word 'love' is as deep as a sea. It permeates every particle of creation. It is directed towards both the animate and inanimate objects. There is no heart that has no love for one thing or the other; but love must be heated like gold and purified of any trace of selfishness; it must be imbued with holiness and be a source of inspiration. Love is the fundamental force in the world and when it reaches its zenith it merges into God. The love and affection cherished by love-sick Mira, Sant Tukaram and that unique love-poet Raskhan burst forth into hymns and prayers. Keep the windows of your heart open to let the breeze of love flow into it and continue to raise it higher and higher to make life natural, simple and stress-free.

Love should be distributed as an offering and benediction to every household. In this world love all, trust few and hate none. The whole life is short for love, then how do people find time to take revenge? Love flourishes on sacrifice and becomes intense when we are willing to give others the utmost we can without expecting anything in return. Love means giving and not receiving. It is synonymous with sacrifice and not with acceptance. In the relationship of give and take, love does not remain love but becomes a deal, on transaction. The heart steeped in love expects no return but believes in making continual sacrifice. The path of love must not be deserted so I wish you to come with me so that you may continue to move on it when I get tired and fail to move forward. Never deviate from the path of love, but steadily stick to it. For this one person should join another person and one heart, another heart and bring every thing under the compass of love.

Love means giving because only those who are willing to give understand the secret of this kindly feeling that generates innumerable traits of personality including intellectual expansion. Through love and sympathy and not through age and intellect can a man peep into another person's mind. 'To hate other is the work of Satan' is a golden saying. Love is a divine quality and to forgive is the duty of man. One who realizes love in his life has a glimpse of God in it.

What Others Say

1. Love, you know, seeks to make happy rather than to be happy. *– Ralph Connor*
2. Love maketh a wit of a fool.
3. Tis better to have loved and lost than never to have loved at all. *– Alfred, Lord Tennyson*
4. Women fall in love through their ears and men through their eyes. *– Woodrow Wyall*
5. Absence sharpens love, presence strengthens it. *– Thomas Fuller*
6. We are all born for love. It is the principle of existence and its only end. *– Disraeli*
7. All true love is grounded on esteem. *– Buckingham*
8. Love is the only glimpse we are permitted of eternity. *– Helen Hayes*

9. There is nothing holier in this life of ours, than the first consciousness of love the first fluttering of its silken wings. Love gives itself, it is not bought.
– Henry Wordsworth Longfellow

10. To love means essentially to give, and to give requires a maturity of self-feeling. *– Rallow May*

11. No cord nor cable can so forcibly draw or hold so fast, as love can do with a twin'd thread. *– Burton*

12. He alone knows love who loves without hope.
– Friedrich Schiller

13. Man is not made for hate and destruction but for love and life. *– S. Radhakrishnan*

14. Pure knowledge and pure love are one and the same. Both lead the aspirants to God. The path of love is much easier. *– Sri Ramakrishna*

15. It is a beautiful necessity of our nature to love something. *– Jerrod*

16. True love begins when nothing is looked for in return.
– Antoine De Saint Exupery

17. Only love can be divided endlessly and still not diminish. *– Anne Morrow Lindbergh*

18. We love those people who give with humility, or who accept with ease. *– Freya Stark*

19. Love conquers all: and we succumb to love. *– Virgil*

20. Love is life and if you miss love, you miss life.
– Leo Buscaglia

21. Love is a canvas furnished by nature and embroidered by imagination.

22. Those who have courage to love should have courage to suffer. *– Anthony Trollope*

Honesty

In simple terms we can say that honesty means that we should do our duty and abstain from everything that does not fall under it. When we do what we are not supposed to do and neglect our duty we are not honest about our work. And from here begins dishonesty. Any work the performance of which gives pleasure and satisfaction to our mind and which is in the interest of family, society and the nation has an element of honesty. Honesty is important both for earning money and for our own conduct. A teacher is honest when he is regular and punctual in teaching in the class room. Expecting a reasonable profit in business is honesty for a businessman and complete dedication to the work of public welfare is honesty for a people's representative. The progress of an honest person may be slow his path may be strewn with obstacles yet it wins people's esteem and praise.

Honesty is an ornament not only for the body alone but for the mind also. The thinking of an honest person is always just. He is the best creation of God and honesty the best policy. An honest businessman may take a long time to become rich but it is certain that he will become rich and also earn public admiration. Only a crafty and deceitful person doubts and denies the existence of honesty. In fact, even dishonesty thrives on honesty. In their personal dealings even the dishonest persons are honest or their association would soon break. If there is a choice between immorality and failure, better opt for failure. Damned be the day, when the thought of earning a single naya paisa with dishonest means crosses the mind of a person.

In the absence of honesty, you cannot lead your life nor can you progress in the direction of spirituality. Honesty is the ethics of life. When you try to be dishonest with an outsider, it portends that your next victim will be your near relation. You will not hesitate in auctioning the dreams of your own people under the hammer of dishonesty. Socially we are leading an artificial and deceitful life and find it difficult to follow the virtues of truth, simplicity and honesty. It is easy to practise honesty but difficult to be deceitful because a dissembler has to concoct a number of lame excuses and speak several tongues. To live an honest life is to lead a natural life because a crafty and treacherous fellow turns the beautiful abode of the spirit into a dustbin of the rubbish of lies.

A dishonest person feels no responsibility towards his family or his society. Remember, the family is the biggest reformatory and it is its duty to check any of its members if he takes to the path of dishonesty. If he is not reformed here even the largest prison-house cannot set him right. The life of an honest person is like a holy book for it gives the eternal message: Be honest and reliable in every situation in your life.

What others say

1. He is not an honest man who has burned his tongue and does not tell the company that the soup is hot.

   – ***Proverb***

2. The genius of communication is the ability to be both totally honest and totally kind at the same time.

   – ***John Powell***

3. Adversity is the trial of principle. Without it, a man hardly knows whether he is honest or not. – ***Henry Fielding***

4. An honest man's word is as good as his bond.

   – ***Cervantes***

5. Being entirely honest with oneself is a good exercise.
– Freud

6. If you do not tell the truth about yourself you cannot tell it about other people. *– Virginia Woolf*

7. It is better to be poor than to be dishonest. *– Bible*

8. It pays to be honest, but it's slow pay. *– Proverb*

9. He that loveth his honesty, has nothing to lose.
– John Lyly

10. An honest man is the noblest work of God. *– Pope*

11. Honesty once pawned is never redeemed.
–Thomas Middleton

Patience

Patience means the capacity to peacefully face adversity. It is the ability to remain undisturbed in unfavourable conditions. Everyone has to face one difficulty or the other in his life everyday. Those who have no forbearance easily give in to them. The strength and endurance that a man evinces in calamitous times speaks of the power of his personality. A man's real strength is tested when he faces misfortune. Patience comes first among the ten characteristics of righteousness.

Only those who are patient, brave and serious-minded continue to make progress in their life and attain their goal. Hence we should practise patience in our life. A virtuous man has said, 'Patience escorts us to the path that leads to the goal of our life. There is nothing else that enables us to do so.' Corroborating this idea, the Hitopadesha says, 'Whether the moralists praise or blame, whether you earn wealth or not, whether death comes today or after a hundred years, the patient persons do not deviate even an inch from the path of justice. Those endowed with such patience are really rich.'

Patience lies at the root of all joy and power because it is fortitude that ascertains half the victory in the battle. Patience is a panacea in the life of man. If we are not calm and contented we shall dig our own grave because nothing less than death can save us from discontent. The soul-force which comes from endurance and fortitude gives us patience. Face every situation without losing your calm and composure. If you wish to have a rose you cannot escape contact with thorns. May be your hand is injured for a time you should not rest until you have plucked the flower.

Those who overlook their goal in face of obstacles or surrender their resolution to pinpricks will never realize their ambition though they make a hundred attempts. Our thinkers are eloquent about the importance of patience in our life. Tulsidas in Ram Charit Manas says:

Patience, righteousness, friendship and your spouse
All are tested in times of calamity.

Indian thought has more highly esteemed the patient than the valiant. It has worshipped them like heroes. Our culture teaches us to adore and decorate patience hundred times more than valour. Our metaphysics, our society and our folk consciousness all address a contented person as a warrior. Ours is the country of the Buddha at whose feet the milk-rice was cooked. It is the country of Mahavir who had his ears nailed. We worship Krishna not because he was a great warrior but because he forgave Bhrigu who had kicked him. We glorify Draupadi for her self-possession and calmness; she forgave the assassin of her five sons to spare his mother the agony she had herself suffered. The greatmen whom we look up to as our ideals believed:

What is there in the path,
And what in the travellers' skill
If it is not strewn with thorns?
What a sailor
And what the test of his patience
If the current is not against him?

To maintain equanimity in times of adversity is true patience. The one who lives it in his life is a real man of fortitude.

What Others Say

1. He that can have patience, can have what he will.
   – ***Benjamin Franklin***
2. Patience is not passive, on the contrary it is active, it is concentrated strength. – ***Bulwer***

3. Patience does not mean indifference, we may work and trust and wait, but we ought not to be idle or careless while waiting. – ***Bulwer***
4. Patience is an ornament to a man, modesty to a woman. – ***Hitopadesha***
5. To be patient under rebuke, and to appear so requires very distinct acts of self-control. – ***Anonymous***
6. Patience and perseverance overcome mountains. – ***Mahatma Gandhi***
7. Patience is the key to contentment. – ***Prophet Mohammad***
8. Our patience will achieve more than our force. – ***Burke***
9. A handful of patience is worth more than a bushel of brains. – ***A proverb***
10. Patience is the companion of wisdom. – ***St. Augustine***
11. Patience and delay achieve more than force and rage. – ***La Fontaine***
12. How poor are they that have not patience! What wound did ever heal but by degrees? – ***Shakespeare***
13. If you are patient in one moment of anger, you will escape a hundred days of sorrow. – ***Chinese Epigram***
14. In any contest between power and patience, bet on patience. – ***W.B. Prescott***
15. Patience is the ability to put up with people you'd like to put down. – ***Ulrike Ruffert***
16. A man without patience is a lamp without oil. – ***Andes Segoria***
17. The greatest prayer is patience. – ***Gautam Buddha***

Satisfaction

Satisfaction is a state in which our mind remains calm and we feel a stream of unique joy flowing there. When contentment enters our mind we lose interest in other means to happiness because contentment is happiness itself. It is a mental state and expresses itself in our conduct and behaviour. We receive our just deserts from God, then what is the use of blindly pursuing desires? These honest and virtuous feelings are what we call satisfaction.

Contentment does not put a check on our aspirations; it opposes only blind desire and covetuousness. We must move forward and rise to great heights, but gradually and in a well-defined way. We should not run breathlessly lest we should stumble. Satisfaction is another name for restraint. It is the greatest pleasure whereas dissatisfaction is the greatest grief. So the one who wants happiness should always remain contented for only a contented person gets the most.

If you are free from jealousy and envy you enjoy supreme contentment. Our mind always hankers after our wants and needs real or imagined. Enjoy whatever you have got; be self-content and thank God as if he has bestowed everything on you. A contented person is self-reliant by nature. When he has filled his small jar rest of the sea water is useless for him. Instead of casting a covetuous glance at the sea waves be tries to quench his thirst. He has no desire to possess the endless sea. Innumerable means of enjoyment lie scattered in the world and it is not possible for any one to collect and command them all. We should get rid of the temptation of possessing anything in excess of what we need for ourselves or for our family. However, we may lay by something for a rainy day. If we are still discontented our mind will know no rest and peace. It will ever be torn by anxiety.

There is a story about King Bhoja who was calm and contented and exercised full control over his mind against temptations. Whatever he could save after meeting the expenses of the state he donated for public welfare. This generous attitude of the King made his treasurer apprehensive. He thought that if the King continued like this one day his treasury would be empty for ever. But he could not dare warn and caution the King so he wrote on a piece of paper 'Save your wealth for a rainy day' and passed it on to the King. Instead of directly replying to him, the King wrote below this line 'Liberal people never expect a rainy day'. The treasurer then wrote, 'What if some day destiny turned against you?' To which the King replied, 'If the destiny turned against me then even the wealth accumulated in the treasury would be lost, so it is not wise to neglect the present duty in a bid to provide for the future.' Think over this reply of the King and you will realize the value of contentment and feel thrilled with a unique joy ever after.

What Others Say

1. Charm is the quality in others that makes us more satisfied with ourselves. *– Henri Frederic Amiel*
2. On the shores of success rises the sun of satisfaction. *–Anonymous*
3. Poor and content is rich and rich enough. *– W. Shakespeare*
4. Contentment is natural wealth, luxury is artificial poverty. *– Socrates*
5. But if I'm content with a little
Enough is as good as a feast. *– Isaac Bickerstaffer*

Glory

Musk is said to be a hundred times more fragrant than saffron, yet the fragrance of glory is even greater than that, for it is the measuring rod of human life. The honour or dishonour you get indicates how the common man estimates you. Good actions are publicly appreciated and bring us honour, or we can say that they serve as the ground work for our honour.

If we are always thinking of the welfare of our family, society and nation and planning our actions accordingly, we are doing good deeds. Our sacrifice makes our actions noble and in this soil of nobility germinate the seeds of our glory. We are honoured for our sacrifice and not for our fraud and deceit. The journey towards glory is not easy; it is arduous like the road to heaven. The path of glory is strewn with thorns. Like poetry and wealth only that glory is good that like the Ganga does good to one and all. This type of glory is admired even by our enemies.

Shruti says that the faces of those who attempt to earn glory by damaging that of the others are blackened so thoroughly that they cannot wash them clean easily. Dishonour is the greatest enemy of man while honour is his best friend. A man of honour enjoys a prominent place in any assembly. Honour pleases all because it imparts power and profit. Our impartial and dignified actions spread fragrance and win honour for us. If you wish to be remembered after your death then either write a popular book or do some memorable deeds. The auspicious acts of a person are appreciated only after some time has lapsed, so you should not expect an immediate recognition of your merit. Reputation like a river begins as a tiny spring at its source but widens later on when it has travelled some distance. If you continue performing noble deeds glory will certainly follow you.

Honour is a man's imperishable possession. The names of Rama, Krishna, Buddha, Mahavira, Jesus and Mohammad are remembered even after thousand years because the deeds they performed were noble and dignified. On the other hand disgraceful acts of the Kauravas, Ravana and Kausa have stained their name for ever. A dying person does not take anything with him. All his wealth cannot save him but the benevolent deeds done by him are ever remembered.

Man thinks that his successors will carry forward his name but it is not so. A man is remembered for the ideals he has lived up to and forgotten if he has been wicked and done mean and contemptible things. The names engraved on stone slabs are soon obliterated but the tale of honour written by a pen of glory continues to impress and inspire people for ages to come. Having your name engraved on stone does not make you great but you become immortal if you sign your name across the heart of the people.

Some people are so hungry for glory that they try to tag their name to it, but it is not possible. Such factitious glory makes a person ridiculous and blurs his vision of life. Good deeds automatically bring in honour, but even an auspicious act gets contaminated if our eyes are fixed on reputation. Steadily stick to a holy and venerable path and glory will follow you as a faithful shadow.

What Others Say

1. The desire for fame tempts even noble minds.

   – St. Augustine

2. Fame is like a river, that beareth up things light and swollen, and downs things weighty and solid.

   – Francis Bacon

3. The celebrity is a person who is known for his well-known-ness. *– Daniel Boorstin*
4. We are all motivated by a keen desire for praise, and the better a man is, the more he is inspired by glory. *– Cicero*
5. There is no business in the world so troublesome as the pursuit of fame, life is over before you have hardly begun your work. *– La Bruyere*
6. There is always room at the top. *– Daniel Webster*
7. Look at everything as though you were seeing it either for the first or the last time. Then your time on earth will be filled with glory. *– Betty Smith*
8. The glory of great men should always be measured by the means they have used to acquire it. *– Francois De La Rochefoucauld*
9. All glory comes from daring to begin. *– Eugene F. Ware*
10. Glory lies in the attempt to reach one's goal and not in reaching it. *– Mahatma Gandhi*
11. The nearest way to glory is to strive to be what you wish to be thought to be. *– Socrates*
12. The road to glory is not strewn with flowers. *– La Fountaine*
13. For glory gives herself only to those who have always dreamed of her. *– Charles De Gaulle*
14. When there is no peril in the fight, there is no glory in the triumph. *– P. Corneille*

Difficulty

Difficulty is really the most difficult word in the dictionary. Beads of sweat appear on a person's forehead as soon as he hears the name of difficulty. Man fears difficulty because he does not understand its psychology. Generally speaking, any obstacle or impediment in the way of performing an action is called difficulty. As there is no road free from obstacles it is not wise to change your path under the fear of difficulties. It is not manly to give in to challenges. The true test of virility consists in changing the direction of winds in your favour. Instead of fearing a difficulty we must manfully face it.

Difficulties test our principles. A man cannot predict whether he is honest or dishonest unless he faces difficulties. Passing through difficult circumstances some people progress very rapidly but some others break down. Remember a stroke of hammer breaks glass but hardens iron into steel. Every difficulty, every misery teaches us something valuable if we are willing to learn it. Many things appear difficult to do in the beginning but our persistent pursuit makes them easy. A poet says:

Neither you, nor we,
But only the conflict is real
Life is not life if it flows
Smooth like water.

Notwithstanding difficulties, the sedulous succeed for they discover a way to overcome them.

There is no difficulty that does not contain its own solution within it. Adversity tests our resolution. No school master is more inexorable than difficulty. Throughout the centuries the wise people have insisted that a brave and noble person never gives in to difficulties but forces them to surrender to him to lay down their arms. The resolution of man dwarfs every difficulty, it makes it bow before him. Difficulty tests our patience. Tulsidasa has rightly said:

Patience, righteousness, friendship and your spouse,
— all are tested in times of adversity.

A calm and contented person is not moved by adversity, he takes it as easily as prosperity. Those who enjoy the days of prosperity should not cry when difficulties befall them. A poet says:

You smiled when happy
Why do you cry in difficulty?
Where the flowers bloom
Thorns also reign there.
Life loves and supports him
Who, on the soil of pain and misery
sows crops of joy.

One who remains steadfast and confident while shedding tears, or enjoying happiness will come out of the difficult days unscathed. We have a psychological problem. As soon as misery overtakes us we stop thinking and start crying whereas the better course would be not to lose heart but to estimate the strength of difficulty. We should then analyze it and try to find out the proper method of resolving it. Sometimes even a speck of difficulty obstructs our thought process and appears as big as a mountain. Sensible and rational people explore and find a path out of difficulties. We should face them steadily and manfully and instead of cowering before them strike a compromise with them. If we comprehend our problems and difficulties, they lose half of their sting.

The best way to solve a difficulty is to find out its nature. When you knock at the door of a cave, there is total darkness inside. Move in slowly and you will see light rising in some corner.

Only hard thinking and not worry brings about this miracle. Instead of pining away with worry and anxiety, think deeply and analyze all the aspects of the problem and you will be surprised that the difficulty that appeared diabolic in discussion and defied solution was nothing more than a trifle.

Rama faced several difficulties during his fourteen years' of exile in the forest. The Pandavas also had the same fate. But they did not cry or faint. They fought the difficulties manfully with confidence and courage and finally overcame them. This is where the brave differ from the ordinary and puerile persons.

Come, let's resolve not to give in to difficulties but, irrespective of their size make them bow before us. I wish to quote a poet:

Shedding tears has not served
anyone in the world.
It's the strong-willed that
have vanquished all calamity.

Now be ready, strengthen your body, mind and will power and then crush every difficulty that dares present itself to you. Make an effort that the difficulty is forced to realize that it made a mistake in chasing you as its victim. Such a resolute person will rise to the occasion and come out victorious.

What Others Say

1. A smooth sea never made a skilful mariner. – ***A proverb***
2. It is difficulties which show what men are. – ***Epictetus***
3. There are no gains without pains. – ***Benjamin Franklin***
4. All things are difficult before they are easy. – ***Thomas Fuller***
5. Difficulties are meant to rouse, not discourage. The human spirit is to grow strong by conflict. – ***William Ellery Channing***
6. Many things difficult to design prove easy to perform. – ***Samuel Johnson***

7. The best way out of a difficulty is through it. – *Anonymous*
8. Difficulty is a severe instructor. – *Burke*
9. The distance is nothing; it is only the first step that is difficult. – *Madame Du Deffand*
10. Ten thousand difficulties do not make one doubt. – *J.H. Newman*
11. Weeping may endure for a might, but joy cometh in the morning. – *Bible*
12. Whom the Lord loveth he chasteneth. – *Bible*
13. Every calamity is a spur and valuable hint. – *R.W. Emerson*
14. There is no wind that always blows a storm. – *Euripides*
15. Problems are only opportunities in work clothes. – *Henry J. Kaiser*
16. If one can really understand the problem, the answer will come out of it, because the answer is not separate from the problem. – *Krishnamurti*
17. Fire is the test of gold, adversity of strong men. – *Seneca*
18. Difficulties vanish when faced boldly. – *Isaac Asimov*
19. Storms make trees take deeper roots. – *Claude Mc Donald*
20. Every problem contains within itself the seeds of its own solution. – *Edward Somers*

Unity

Unity is a word that draws our attention to the collective force. But collective force does not simply come from a collection of people. We cannot bind a crowd of people in a string of unity because the crowd has no ideational relationship with one another but unity depends on this ideational relationship alone. In other words we can say that agreement at the level of feeling or action on a particular subject makes for unity. Unity is essential for public welfare. Unity is strength. In fact, nothing worthwhile can be achieved in its absence. Beginning with the family, unity spreads to society, nation and the whole world. It does not stand for merger but strength, excellence and wakefulness. The trees growing in a clump can stand the fiercest storm because they support each other whereas a single tree, howsoever, strong it might be is felled in a trice.

Unity means that we have one aim, one object and join each other in pleasure and pain. All should function like the fingers on the palm which whether large or small join together and make a collective effort when lifting an object. They are five in number but perform thousands of actions when they are united. Selfishness should not blind our love. We should move together neck with neck, shoulder with shoulder and foot with foot taking care that our heads do not collide.

When we develop such unity we can realize all our dreams. Various organizations should not cherish differences between themselves because if the mutual differences intensify unity becomes difficult. Often we find that organizations split, families break, and parties pull apart in a rupture because of slight differences on the ideational level. Initially we admit and condone differences under the misapprehension that democracy sanctions them. The right thing would be that we sit together and sort out our differences without a clash of egos for the clash of egos shakes the foundation of unity. When every brick begins to crumble and fall apart talking of the strength of the wall has no meaning. This applies to institutions, organizations, families and society as well.

When the strands of unity begin to untwist the warp and woof of the organization becomes loose and one day all the tissues and yarns scatter. To stop this process of disintegration we need sacrifice and mutual understanding. Unless we are willing to relinquish our point of view for the good of the community our unity will not last. We should act on the principle 'One for all and all for one'. In the absence of mutual understanding we cannot digest the apparent differences. We must, therefore, widen the horizon of our understanding. When we make a sincere attempt to understand the feelings of others the possibility of unity will become a ground reality.

What Others Say

1. If a house be divided against itself that house cannot stand. – ***Bible***
2. A three-fold cord is not quickly broken. – ***Ecclesiastes***
3. Behold, how good and how pleasant, it is for brethren to dwell together in unity. – ***Psalm 133:1***
4. We must all hang together, or we shall all hang separately. – ***Benjamin Franklin***
5. Weak things united become strong.
6. If a link is broken, the whole chain breaks. – ***Yiddish proverb***

Vision

According to a thinker the two main streams of a man's life in this world are vision and creation. Vision consists of a man's thinking and meditation, his thoughts, beliefs and feelings which regulate his development. Creation includes a man's life style and his manners and customs etc. Creation is construction and when vision enters creation it brings forth civilization and culture.

Man is endowed with both vision and creation so the question arises which of these he should change first and where to start the process. Some theorists advise that he should change the creation first. It means that he should change his life style, manners and customs and renovate himself, his family and society. He should control both his own life and that of the world.

On the other hand Indian philosophers have always insisted on a change of vision first because a man's development is incongruous unless he changes his attitude. If he does not raise his vision from a lower plane to a higher one or does not turn it from the worldly pleasures to the joy of salvation, he cannot bring about a change in his life.

Religion also holds that first we should change vision and then creation. That is first we must change our ideas and then our conduct. This view may surprise some because man expresses his real self-through his conduct. But conduct by itself is not free to perform even the smallest action because it is like a horse harnessed to a chariot which is controlled by a driver. Mind is that invisible driver who with a whip of ideas controls the horse of conduct. If we wish the horse to take the right path then before controlling its speed we should discipline the driver and make him conscientious because the change of conduct is meaningful only if it results from a change in ideas.

It will be futile to change the creation without first changing the vision. It applies to the scriptures also. In themselves they are neither good nor bad. It is the man's vision that interprets them the either way. A vicious person steeped in sensual pleasures uses scriptures as a weapon of destruction. If one studies a principle without first changing his vision he might misuse it to harm others.

Milk is a source of nutrition. It replenishes the loss of bodily energy and is useful for old and young alike. But if it is given to a person suffering from indigestion, it will worsen his condition. Same is the case with purified butter which strengthens a healthy person but acts as a poison for the one suffering from liver trouble. Similarly, if the vision is vitiated even good ideas would be perverted and mis-employed.

Unless the mirror of your mind and vision is clear it will not present a true reflection of your life. You will not recognize who you are. If your vision is blurred no scripture will help you to see yourself.

If you wish to revolutionize your life understand your inner self. It will give you equanimity. All religions have unanimously stated that when the soul is sturdy it convokes the courage to call a spade a spade and find out what is iniquitous in our thought, word and deed. Then we can forcibly extricate the immorality lying long buried in the depth of our inner self. And for this we need a jerk of renunciation in our conduct, for only the conduct which is an expression of wakefulness is fruitful in life.

What Others Say

1. Vision is the art of seeing things invisible.
   – Jonathan Swift

2. Where there is no vision, the people perish.
   – Proverbs 29:18

3. Nothing ever built arose to touch the skies unless someone dreamed that it should, believed that it could and someone willed that it must. *– A Schweitzer*

4. Reason may fail you. If you are going to do anything with life, you must sometimes follow visions and dreams.
   – Bede Jarrett

5. People see only what they are prepared to see.
   – R.W. Emerson

6. Only he who keeps his eye fixed on the far horizon will find his right road. *– Dag Hammarskjold*

7. A moment's insight is sometimes worth a life's experience. *– Oliver Wendell Holmes*

8. I believe in the imagination. What I cannot see is infinitely more important than what I can see. *– Duane Michals*

9. It is only with the heart that one can see rightly; what is essential is invisible to the eye.
   – Antoine De Saint Exupery

10. The man who insists upon seeing with perfect clearness before he decides, never decides.
    – Henri Frederic Amiel

11. A great teacher never strives to explain his vision. He simply invites you to stand beside him and see for yourself. *– Rev. R. Inman*

Company

The ideal of the ancient Vedic life is: Live together and think at the same level. Dine together, treat all as equals and work together for the rise of one and all. This will bring about the welfare of all. This human tendency to come closer is called company. In plain terms company means living together, moving together, conversing together as well as acting and behaving together. Company changes the condition and direction of life. Good company like a physician or a medicine cures incurable mental diseases. Hence we should exercise discretion while selecting our companions.

Living in good company has its own advantage. It pleases like perfume and that too in gratis. It is good pastime and helps in exchange of good ideas, good actions and good feelings. It enables us to know and understand God and move towards Him. Our culture gives a clarion call: Let your companions be gentle folk, avoid the company of the wicked, for those who teach you evil things and evil habits do not deserve to be your friends.

If your companions are men of low and mean mentality they will make you also to stoop low. In the company of equals we maintain equanimity; we neither rise above nor fall down. In the company of the noble we develop our intellect and move upwards. Kabir has rightly said:

Kabira says the company of the gentle
is like that of a perfumer.
He might not give us anything concrete,
but can't hold back his perfume.

A thinker says: Tell me who your companions are and I shall tell you what you are. A man's movement, countenance and character all are moulded by his company. The company of the well-behaved persons makes him creative. Whereas the company of the wicked writes his down fall. A thinker has gone to the extent of saying: Never mind if you have some evil habit but never entertain the company of the wicked. You may get rid of your evil habit one day, but an evil company will drag you for ever into the bylanes of crime.

It is said that in the company of the depraved even a gentleman loses his value as an expensive wreath placed on a dead body loses all its worth. Company matters not only for human beings but for birds and animals too.

A parrot or a myna kept as a pet by a gentleman repeats the name of God whereas the one kept by a villain utters words of abuse. In the journey of life man faces many ups and downs. Here the role of his fellow travellers is very important; if they are kind and cheerful, they will convert the evil into good but if they are corrupt and sinful they will rob him of all his uprightness. Our conduct is affected by our company to a large extent. A man should develop the faculty to discriminate good from the bad company. If we wish to behave in a civilized, noble and charming manner we should keep company only with the people who make our life clean and virtuous.

It is why all religions are so eloquent about the worth of good company. Tulsidas is absolutely correct when he says that in the absence of the company of the upright people we cannot develop our power of reasoning and discrimination. Good company like a detergent washes our life clean both inside and outside. Have friends whose company helps you improve your character. Company is the work-shop where you can design your life in the way you like.

What Others Say

1. A pleasant companion reduces the length of the journey. *– Syrus*
2. A man is better known by the company he keeps. *– Anonymous*
3. Man loves company even if it is only that of a small burning candle. *– Georg Christoph Lichtenberg*
4. The companionship of the holy and the wise is one of the main elements of spiritual progress. *– Sri Ramakrishna*
5. Associate yourself with men of good quality, if you esteem your own reputation, for it is better to be alone than to be in bad company. *– George Washington*
6. Avoid the man of temper, the selfish, the boastful, the scornful, the liar, lest you acquire his ways of thinking. *– Anonymous*
7. Good company and discourse are the very sinews of virtue. *– Izaak Walton*
8. Birds of a feather flock together.
9. When a dove begins to associate with crows, its feathers remain white but its heart grows black. *– German proverb*
10. He that walketh with wise men shall be wise. *– Proverbs 13:20*
11. He that lies down with dogs will rise up with fleas. *– Latin proverb*
12. A crowd is not company, and faces are but a gallery of pictures, and talk but a tinkling cymbal, where there is no love. *– Bacon*
13. My idea of good company is the company of clever, well-informed people who have a great deal of conversation. *– Jane Austen*
15. Few are qualified to shine in company, but it is in most men's power to be agreeable. *– Johathan Swift*

Gentleness

Gentleness is a natural quality. It is the inborn nature of man. It is not acquired but has to be cultivated. The gentleness which is acquired with deliberate effort is not real gentleness but only a mask, a display, a disguise. If a man really wants to become gentle he must form the habit of identifying his interest with the public good. A true gentleman lives with honesty and courtesy, works for the welfare of others, keeps himself away from evil tendencies, is steeped in devotion to God and maintains perfect harmony with his family and society.

A gentleman is generosity and courteousness incarnate and provides guidance to humanity. A gentleman is equated with a saint. A thinker has rightly said: I don't expect to meet a saint today, but I shall feel amply rewarded even if I run into a gentleman. Gentlemen spread love, goodwill and noble-mindedness in society. A poet has rightly said:

Nobility breeds love and love breeds happiness
Flowers emanate fragrance which attracts bees.

A gentleman is not distressed by penury nor is he elated by wealth. It is said that if a rich man is gentle, his wealth is well-meaning. Be polite with all, but intimate with few, and confide in only a selected minority duly tested. A gentleman is like sandalwood. Burn it, cut it, shave or scrape it, it always gives fragrance but it does not mean that a gentleman should be deliberately harassed. You will be punished by God if you do so. A gentleman behaves in a peculiar way. He does not misuse his wealth, never boasts of his family, but keeps to the path of benevolence and is charitable by nature.

Gentle people are resolute and never waver from the path of politeness in face of innumerable calamities. They don't give up their civility even when the wicked torture them. There is a well-known saying: At the end of this era Mount Sumeru may move, the seven seas may cross their boundary but a gentleman will never flinch even an inch from his resolution and promise. Such gentle people behave like deities though living in the shape of human beings. Even gods descend on the earth to catch a glimpse of them. A poet has rightly said:

The world will become pious and fragrant,
When man begins to behave as man.

Man pretends to be an angel but does not try even to become a man in the true sense. The day manliness dawns on man, he will in no way remain less than an angel. A man can become a man if the feelings of gentlemanliness rise in his heart.

Man can be both an animal and a god. He is an animal when inauspicious tendencies arise in his mind and he is a god when he is charitable and benevolent. A man must raise his mental level. If our mind continues wandering in sensual and gross pleasures, avarice, rage and egoism we will become fiercer than a wild beast. Make your mind a garden and let the flowers of gentleness, nobility and benevolence blossom there to create a totally new environment which will make everyone a gentleman. If we are able to do so our life will be worthwhile and present an ideal for the world.

What Others Say

1. Propriety of manners and consideration for others are the two main characteristics of a gentleman.

   – Benjamin Disraeli

2. A gentleman is one who never insults anyone intentionally.

3. A gentleman respects even those who can be of no possible value to him. He never hurts anyone's feelings intentionally. *– Phelps and Herford*

4. A true gentleman carefully avoids all clashing of opinion, or collision of feeling, his great concern being to make everyone at their ease and at home. He is never mean or little in his disputes, never takes unfair advantage. He is patient, forbearing and resigned. He submits to pain because it is inevitable, and to death, because it is his destiny. *– Cardinal Newman*

5. There is nothing stronger in the world than gentleness. *– Han Suyin*

6. How sweet it is when the strong are also gentle! *– Libbie Fudim*

7. Feelings are every where – be gentle. *– J. Masai*

Time

Time is a bird that never looks back when once in flight, but continues flying. The time bird is not destined to perch on a branch and rest. Time is a traveller that never gets tired of journeying. Neither adversity nor prosperity can stop its flight. It is always flying, marching on. In his life a man faces delight and happiness as well as misery and misfortune. When we accomplish our plans and earn easy profit we feel delighted and call it good time. But when there is an adverse turn in life and we suffer loss we feel miserable and say the time is not good.

In itself time is neither good nor bad. We evaluate it on the basis of our success or failure and call it favourable or unfavourable. If something is wrong today tomorrow it may be right. Even if the time is unfavourable we should patiently wait for it to take a favourable turn, for time and tide wait for none. We should not waste time because it is the stuff our life is made of. It is a non-stop watch that always keeps on running. However, limited may be the time at our disposal, it becomes shorter if we waste it. Spend so much time on your self-improvement that none is left for harming others because it is possible, though with dogged effort to retrieve health, wealth and honour if they slip from our hands but the time that has once slipped past can never be brought back. A river flows on and never returns. Similarly, day follows night and the life of man draws to a close. During the course of life two things might happen either we lose our status, possessions, wealth and youth while still living or we depart this life leaving them all behind. The best way of making fortune smile on us is to make proper use of every moment of our life. Wasting time means wasting our life.

The treasures of the world are insignificant before time even the strongest person has to stoop at the altar of time. Proper utilization of time is a positive gain and its misuse an invitation to disaster. The one who is wakeful about the fleeting nature of time does not put off anything for tomorrow. A thinker goes to the extent of saying, 'If you finish in twenty four hours what you normally do in forty eight hours, you double your life span'. Those who proceed on the path of life with this thought in mind leave their footprints on the sand of time. The fairy called success crowns them.

What Others Say

1. The time is always right to do what is right. *– Rev. Martin Luther King Jr.*
2. Love and time-those are the only two things in all the world and all of life that cannot be bought, but only spent. *– Gery Jennings*
3. Time wastes our bodies and our wits, but we waste ;time, so we are quits. *– Verse and Worse*
4. How you spend your time is more important than how you spend your money. Money mistakes can be corrected, but time is gone for ever. *– David B. Nonis*
5. When we don't waste time, we always have enough. *– Jean Drapeau*
6. You can't make footprints in the sands of time sitting down.
7. Time gives good advice. *– Maltese Proverb*
8. Don't thou love life? Then do not squander time, for that's the stuff life is made of. *– Benjamin Franklin*
9. All the treasures of earth cannot bring back one lost moment. *– French Proverb*
10. Time is the wisest of all counselors. *– Plutarch*

11. Those who make the worst use of their time most complain of its shortness. – ***La Bruyere***
12. Time misspent is not lived but lost. – ***Thomas Fuller***
13. He most lives who thinks most, feels the noblest, acts the best. – ***Gamallel Balley***
14. Those who have most to do, and are willing to work, will find the most time. – ***Samuel Smiles***
15. Time discovrs the truth. – ***Seneca***
16. Time will change for the better when you change. – ***Anonymous***
17. A day once gone will never return. Therefore, one should be diligent each moment to do good. We reach the goal of good life by pious work. – ***Mahavira***
18. The poison of panic grows in 'yesterdays'. The flower of felicity grows in 'tomorrows'. Make all your 'tomorrows happy' today's, so that your life will be long and healthy, successful and vital. – ***Walter M Germain***
19. Time brings all things to pass. – ***Aeschylus***
20. Time flies over us, but leaves its shadow behind. – ***Nathaniel Hawthorne***
21. Ordinary people merely think how they shall spend time, a man of intellect tries to use it. – ***Arthur Schopenhauer***

Advice

The teachings based on a well-informed person's wisdom and experience are called advice. Others need not give us advice; we can get it from our own daily behaviour and experience. However, the adviser should invariably remember whom he is advising and in what circumstances. Sometimes advice may cause bitterness. Teachings, suggestions or advice should be given in private keeping in view the self-respect of the recipient. It can not be disputed that right type of advice given at a right time and in a right manner may even change the course of our life.

To give advice is not only the prerogative of the elderly persons; even a small child can do so. A clay lamp becomes all important after the sun set. Similarly, with his timely advice a small child can help us get out of miserable circumstances. Our classical literature is full of examples where a dog, a pig, a cat or even small insects have given us silent advice.

Your advice will not be effective unless your own life is upright. When you practise what you preach others to do, your advice acts as purifying holy water of the Ganga; but if it is just a theoretical proposition on which you do not act yourself, it will have no influence on your listeners.

It is seen that political and religions leaders often talk of making sacrifices or even immolating themselves, but their advice always falls flat. Every political leader wishes that children like Bhagat Singh be born in every family except his own for they would be executed. Every father wishes his son to be Rama but he himself is not willing to become Dasharatha who redeemed his word and sent his beloved son into the forest when preparations for his coronation were in full swing. Can the crafty religions leaders of today do so? The answer is a definite 'No'.

At a time when accidents are happening all round us it will be better if we make our life a source of inspiration so that others willingly follow in our foot steps. The advice of those who lead such an ideal life can change the nation's destiny.

What Others Say

1. I have found that the best way to give advice to your children is to find out what they want, and then advise them to do it. – ***Henry S. Truman***
2. I sometimes give myself admirable advice, but I am incapable of taking it. – ***Mary Wortley Montagu***
3. To profit from good advice requires more wisdom than to give it. – ***John Churton Collins.***
4. A knife of the keenest steel requires the whetstone, and the wisest man needs advice. – ***Zoroaster***
5. When we are well, we have good advice for those who are ill. – ***Terence***
6. Advice is an uncertain gift. – ***W. Jeffrey***
7. I can easier teach twenty what were good to be done than be one of the twenty to follow my own teaching. – ***Anonymous***
8. Many receive advice, only the wise profit by it. – ***Pulitius Syrus***
9. Advice is judged by results, not be intentions. – ***M.T. Cicero***
10. One who is not wise himself cannot be well-advised. – ***Nicco Lo Machiavelli***

11. If a man loves to give advice, it is a sure sign that he himself wants it. – ***Lord Halifax***

12. The worst men often give the best advice.
– ***Phillip J. Baily***

13. He that gives good advice, builds with one hand; he that gives good counsel and example, builds with both.
– ***Bacon***

14. Never give advice in a crowd. – ***Arab Proverb***

15. Advice is like snow, the softer it falls, the longer it dwells upon, and the deeper it sinks into the mind.
– ***S.T. Coleridge***

16. Advice is seldom welcome, and those who want it the most always like it the least. – ***Earl of Chesterfield***

Nation

A Nation is not just a distinct territory. It is a cultural concept that finds expression in religion, society, manners, literature and constancy in public life. It symbolizes an ideological unity that binds the citizens together notwithstanding their diversity and disparity. We may have differences in language, dress and food habits, but nationalism, the spirit of a nation is the bond that fastens all of us together. This spiritual fidelity that sustains life may be termed our nationality.

No doubt nation stands for a definite piece of land where people live, have their government and enjoy independence. The affinity and intimacy that we develop for the land where we are born and brought up and where our life blossoms forth is called our nationality. It is the love for the nation that makes us identify its dignity and glory with our dignity and glory, its culture as our culture and exhorts us to defend, foster and cherish them and make constant efforts for their evolution.

We should cherish the same duty, feel the same reverence and honour for our motherland as we do for our mother. Mother and motherland are placed even above paradise. Love and friendship for the vast family of mankind enables us to grow and imparts real strength to the nation. A nation cannot stand united in the absence of fellow feeling among its citizens. The mutual goodwill supplies brick and mortal for the building of a nation, but discord and disparity shake its very foundation. A poet has rightly said:

Divide not the nation into tribes
Divide not the journey into miles
Our country is a river inviolate
Divide it not into ponds and lakes.

Duty towards nation is the highest civil duty. Citizens in a nation may follow any mode or way of worship, but in praising the nation they all join together and raise their voice in unison. Followers of all religions in our country keep their national duty above all differences. India is a land of many languages, many customs and manners, hundreds of religious faiths. Indian civilization has strands of many civilizations that give it a multicolored texture. Inspite of several races, castes and sub-castes the collective consciousness that binds every citizen in the country, makes up our nationalism.

As a reaction to the divisive tendencies that are driving people away from their national duty we have to suffer at the hands of the demon of terrorism. The attempt to obliterate the diversity in a bid to create uniformity gives rise to several social anomalies. We sing the song of unity in several languages. A variety of religions faiths represents evolution and expansion of our spirituality. Different dresses display our internal joy and happiness. Geographically the country is so vast that we have one of the six seasons throughout the year in one part or the other. Europe is cold and snow covered for most of the year, Arab deserts blaze in summer heat but winter, summer, rainy season and spring visit India on schedule.

Our sages have seen cultural unity in the flow of rivers, discerned gods and goddesses in hills and mountains, watched the playful activities of the Lord in each and every particle of land. Our centres of pilgrimage in east and west, north and south speak of our spiritual unity. Our country has provided asylum even to her enemies and tolerance we have superb. Whatever religion, culture, literature, language, art that entered our country got itself assimilated with what was already flourishing here. We have raised the slogan 'The whole world is a family'. Can anyone think of a country where people with so many differences live so cordially? Truly, India is a great nation. We should willingly sacrifice all we have to become worthy members of it and only then we can claim to be called true and good Indians.

What Others Say

1. A nation's work never ends. Men may come and go, generations may pass but the life of a nation goes on.
   – Jawaharlal Nehru
2. A nation reveals itself not only by the men it produces, but also by the men it honours, the men it remembers.
   – John F. Kennedy
3. Nations get as good or as bad a government as they deserve. ***– Allen Hume***
4. the worth of a state in the long run, is the worth of the individuals composing it. ***– John Stewart Mill***
5. A nation without means of reform is a nation without means of survival. ***– Edmund Burke***
6. Nations, like individuals, are made, not only by what they acquire but by what they resign.
   – S. Radhakrishanan
7. The destiny of any nation at any given time depends on the opinion of its young men under five and twenty.
   – J.W.Goethe
8. Not with dreams but with blood and iron, shall a nation be moulded at last. ***– Algernon Charles Swinburns***
9. No one loves his country for its size, or eminence, but because it is his own. ***– Seneca***
10. It is a sweet and seemly thing to die for one's country.
    – Horace
11. Ask not what your country can do for you, ask what you can do for your country. ***– John F. Kennedy***

12. Patriotism is not so much protecting the land of our fathers as preserving the land of our children.

    – Jose Ortega Y. Gasset

13. A country free enough to examine its own conscience is a land worth living in, a nation to be envied.

    – Prince Charles

14. A people that values its privileges above its principles soon loses both. *– D.D. Eisenhower*

15. To understand a man, you must know his memories. The same is true of a nation. *– Anthony Quayle*

16. The life of the nation is secure only while the nation is honest, truthful and virtuous. *– Frederick Douglass.*

Relations

Relations string people into family and when a number of families join together we have a community. Social communities coalesce to form castes and when a number of caste groups come closer they lay the foundation of the nation. The world is an aggregate of nations. Thus it is the string of relations that brings not only individuals but also societies together and serves as a cohesive force. Ancient Indian scriptures emphasized the idea that the whole world is a family.

The sphere of relations has shrunk today; they are now limited to blood relations or at the most include some very close and intimate friends. Now let us consider how best we can define relations. Generally speaking, relations are emotional in nature and signify the way people behave together. For example, parents, siblings and other members of a family have blood relations. Family and some social groups are essentially based on blood relations. Secular relations depend on mutual interest and as soon as our purpose is served we withdraw from them.

The texture of relations begins to give in when we distrust each other, entertain diverse views or begin to exploit others to gain our selfish ends. Disintegration starts and bitterness replaces harmony. Secular relations survive on truth and honesty but we must have faith and confidence to establish relationship with God.

In the present day we feel a momentary warmth of relations and very soon they begin to fester and stink like wet wounds. Sincere relations flourish on the soil of generosity. In the absence of dedication the spring of love dries up. Affection, good will and sensitiveness are the elements that lead the relations to their fulfilment whereas the relations based on selfishness are ephemeral like a line drawn on water. True relation is an indelible line inscribed on stone.

Today the atmosphere in the world is heavy with growing conflict and weariness; man is raising walls of hatred and revenge and feelings of retaliation fill the world. To gain his petty interests man has forgotten the sanctity of relations. The subversion of relations not only corrupts the inner-self of man but also prepares ground for the disintegration of family. This is why the joint family system is dying out slowly. Selfishness has so blind-folded man that the interests of mother and son, husband and wife, father and son and brothers are clashing and they feel alienated from each other. A poet has rightly said:

Since you raised a wall
in the heart's courtyard
the bricks of hatred have
crushed the tiny plant of love.
Avoid breaking someone's heart
with your sarcastic remarks
for it is a temple where the
Lord has his abode.

To make your inner-self pure and holy raise your secular relations on a pious and liberal foundation.

All our saints and seers hold that we are the children of God. If we cherish for all the creatures in the world the same affectionate intimacy that we feel for our blood relations the whole world will become a large extended family. If we share the joy and sorrow of every member of society we shall strengthen our temporal bonds and transform them into permanent relations. God expects us to have the same unflinching love for Him. We must try to win the love of all and shower our love on them.

This will create an atmosphere of faith and trust and transform the world into paradise.

What Others Say

1. We begin our public affections in our families. No cold relation is a zealous citizen. *– Edmund Burke*
2. A sense of duty is useful in work, but offensive in personal relations. People wish to be liked, not to be endured with patient resignation. *– Bertrand Russell*
3. Always do what you say you are going to do. It is the glue and fibre that binds successful relationships. *– Jeffry A. Timmons*
4. Getting people to like you is only the other side of liking them. *– Norman Vincent Peale*
5. It's the things in common that make relationships enjoyable, but it's the little differences that make them interesting. *– Todd Ruthman*
6. What do we live for if it is not to make life less difficult for each other. *– George Eliot*
7. The ultimate test of a relationship is to disagree but to hold hands. *– Alexandra Penney*
8. The greatest of all arts is the art of living together. *– William Lyons Phelps*
9. A happy family is but an earlier heaven. *– John Bowring*
10. A relationship is like a diamond, which has to be cut and polished to enhance its lust and beauty. *– Rabindranath Tagore*
11. Community is simply the fullness of home. *– Paul Hinnebusch*
12. The community stagnates without the impulse of the individual. The impulse dies without the sympathy of the community. *– William James*

Mother

Indian culture equates mother with deities but the significance of mother is even more than gods because the incarnations, tirthankars, prophets and saints all grow and play in the lap of mother and enjoy heavenly bliss there. Among all the invaluable relations in the world the one with mother is the holiest and most unselfish. She gives us birth. There is no alternative, no synonym for her. It is the mother who first feels the pleasure and pain of the child. Her affection for the child whom she carries in her womb for nine months is as holy as her milk.

She performs the arduous task of building the character of the child and socializing him. She is the living image of God and at her feet we feel the happiness of all the three worlds. She must be honoured, nay worshipped. All the joys and pleasures of the world pale into insignificance before her natural love and affection. She is tenderness, holiness and infinite affection incarnate. The joy we get in her arms, the peace we get crying under her scarf, the ineffable bliss we feel in her affectionate touch can only be experienced at the level of spirit.

Sacrifice, patience and love together with tenderness and piety are the ingredients used by God to create the image of mother.

It is said that a spiritual teacher is more valuable than ten secular teachers, a father more than ten spiritual teachers but the rank of mother is even greater than one thousand fathers. There is a difference between the mother's affection and the comforts of the household. The one is a sea of cool water and the other a desert. We must consecrate the mother's image in the temple of our heart. She is worth the holiest pilgrimage and to serve and worship her is more sacred and holier than visiting all the places of pilgrimage. The one who is careful not to inflict any pain on his mother will lead a trouble free life. The debt we owe to our mother, though irrepayable can be redeemed to some extent by serving her. So the scriptures again and again remind us our duty to our mother. A poet says:

Why to worry to see the one
Who is invisible!
Mother represents on earth
The image of God.

Mother, father and teacher are the three visible and tangible gods. Worshipping the invisible and intangible gods to the neglect of these three can never be justified. Our culture refers to gods and goddesses as father and mother. We call God the Supreme Father, and see the glimpse of our mother in the goddesses. Our mother is not only Laxmi, Saraswati or Durga but even above them. Hence we address our country as our motherland. Mother's heart is deep like the sea and her spirit vast like the sky.

Motherhood is not just a relationship but a feeling and to make ourselves like our mother we should offer all our wealth at her feet. In the changed circumstances of today those who ill-treat their mother should take a lesson from the life of Rama who preferred exile to his coronation just to please his stepmother.

The definition of family today has become very narrow and shallow because today only parents and their minor children form part of it. A mother can easily raise five children, but it is regrettable that five children cannot join together to take care of their mother. There was a time when children lived with their parents, but today the parents long to live with their children.

The present generation under the impact of western culture considers that its duty is done just by presenting to their mother a greeting card and a bouquet on 'mother's day'. Our culture is mother oriented. We address nature, a river and the earth as mother. We start our day by singing praises of mother in the morning. How sad it is that the mother who is so much at the centre of our life is denied a place even in the corner of the house. Is it not the limit of our cultural down fall?

But there is no need to feel frustrated; it is never too late to make amends. Let us start searching our roots at our mother' feet. In will be a great day when we realize the importance of mother. It will be sheer foolishness to unravel the secret of life before first understanding the feelings of the one who brought us forth into this world. Come, let us dedicate ourselves to the great ideal of serving the mother and seek her blessings for peace and prosperity in the world.

What Others Say

1. Youth fades, love drops, the leaves of friendship fall. A mother's secret hope outlives them all. ***– O.W. Holmes***
2. Mother is the name for God in the lips and hearts of children. ***– W.M. Thackeray***
3. God could not be everywhere so he made mothers. ***– Anonymous***
4. The future destiny of the child is always the work of the mother. ***– Napoleon Bonaparte***
5. The best academy, a mother's knee. ***– J.R. Lowell***
6. One mother can take care of ten children, but ten children can't take care of one mother.
7. All that I am, or I hope to be, I owe to my angel mother. ***– Abraham Lincoln***
8. What is home without a mother? ***– Alice Hawthorne***

Marriage

Indian tradition put a spiritual interpretation on the relationship between a husband and wife. In our social structure, a wife is not only a house maker but a religiously sanctified companion. No religious rite or ceremony can be performed in her absence. She is not only the better half of man but also occupies half his body and carries half of man in her own body. She is a test of his manliness which is proved in the gentle arms of a well-behaved and satisfied wife.

Among the four goals of human life – righteousness, wealth, desire and salvation–desire for sex comes third. Its fulfilment is essential for physical pleasure and race procreation. The institution of marriage was created to cater to this desire and the loving couple was accorded social acceptance as husband and wife.

In India marriage is a religious ritual and ceremony and not a social contract. It is the meeting of two souls which continues from one birth to another. The relation between a husband and wife becomes enjoyable if they understand each other's feelings and respect them, make sacrifice for each other, provide mutual enjoyment and take care of each other in times of joy and sorrow.

With the changing times social concepts are undergoing a rapid change. A wife now desires equal rights and respect. The status of a man entitles his wife to receive respect because he is her master and guide. The wife is the better half and the best friend of her husband. If a man lags behind his companions on the path of life his wife gives him company. We cannot imagine a household in her absence. A householder is not one who lives in a house but one who lives with his wife whose presence makes it a household and her absence a barren forest. The duty of a husband is to support and protect his wife and in return the wife should provide him true enjoyment to justify her name. Basically, their relationship is truly spiritual. A man forgets all his pain and fatigue if his wife welcomes him with a smile when he returns home, lovingly enquires about his business and offers him food and drink.

At present the relationship between a husband and wife has changed and they behave like two parallel lines which move together but never meet. This false sense of equality has loosened the structure of the family because the husband and wife are the pivots round which the family chariot rotates. Today the pivots have been shaken and thrown out of alignment; hence it is not surprising if the chariot of household has lost its equilibrium. Today they treat each other only as man and woman hence the relationship of a husband and wife fails to grow between them. Husband and wife should identify with each other. The relationship between man and woman that aims at sensual gratification only is superficial and short-lived. It has no spiritual foundation and lacks the warmth and glow of the Supreme Creator.

The relationship between a husband and wife is the best representation of human sensibilities. Unfortunately, today it has become mechanical instead of emotional, which has created chaos not only in married life but in the whole social structure. To revive this tender and sweet relationship of mutual affection people should search for the sweet aroma of sacrifice before fighting for the rights of a husband or a wife.

What others say

1. Those marriages generally abound most with love and constancy that are preceded by a long courtship. *– Joseph Addison*
2. Marriage is a result of the longing for the deep, deep peace of a settled life after the chase of the opposite sex. *– Anonymous*
3. A single man is an incomplete animal. He resembles the odd half of a pair of scissors. *– Benjamin Franklin*
4. Faithful women are all alike. They think only of their fidelity and not of their husbands'. *– Jean Giraudoux*
5. There is no more lovely, friendly, and charming relationship, communion or company than a good marriage. *– Martin Luther*
6. A good marriage is that in which each appoints the other the guardian of his solitude. *– Rainer Maria Rilke*
7. It is a woman's business to get married as soon as possible, and a man's to keep unmarried as long as he can. *– George Bunard Shaw*
8. Marriage is popular because it combines the maximum of temptation with the maximum of opportunity. *– G.B. Shaw*
9. Marriage is the greatest earthly happiness when founded on complete sympathy. *– Benjamin Disraeli.*
10. Wives are young men's mistress, companions for middle age and old men's nurses. *– Francis Bacon*
11. The first bond of society is marriage. *– Cicero*
12. The happiness of married life depends upon making small sacrifices with readiness and cheerfulness. *– Selden*
13. Marriage is the great civilizer of the world. *– Robert Hall*
14. For a successful marriage, both sides must share equal responsibilities. *– Anonymous*
15. Marriage resembles a pair of shears, so joined that they cannot be separated, often moving in opposite directions, yet always punishing anyone who comes between them. *– Sydney Smith*

Woman

The Sanskrit word for woman (Nari) literally means 'one who has no enemies, the one who is ever loveable'. As a sweet daughter, she is a toy and as a sister an ornament. As a mother she transcends heaven and as a wife, forms one half of man. She is the fairest creation of God. Streams of affection, liberality and sensitiveness are intertwined in the form of a woman. She is imbued with other qualities also; she is emotional, pious and magnanimous and creative by nature.

Woman enters the life of man as a puff of gentle breeze. In fact, without her not only the life of man but that of the whole universe is incomplete. She is power, devotion, affection and asceticism all rolled into one. She must be looked at with reverence and not displayed, must be worshipped in the temple of heart and not physically exploited. After God, we owe her the greatest debt. She not only brings us forth into the world but trains us to live a successful life.

A woman is like the shadow of man, if you run after her she recedes but if you run away from her she follows. Beauty may make a woman proud but when she cultivates good qualities she is adored. Modesty makes her a veritable goddess. She is wiser than man, though she knows less, she understands more. As flowers adorn a thorny branch a fair but modest woman turns the poorest home into a paradise.

Modesty multiplies her beauty a hundred times, it is a crucial fact, for the gem of her beauty remains safe in the invincible chest of modesty. Today woman is aping to be a butterfly.

Fashion has so overpowered her that she always floats in the world of imagination has lost contact with hard ground realities. There is hue and cry that the media is exposing her body for the sake of advertisement. It may be true but the other painful aspect of this truth is that she is willingly exposing herself before the eye of the camera. Unless a woman regains her self-respect she cannot be withdrawn from the market place.

Our culture allows woman full liberty but no license. A woman should take a turn towards her godliness; she is power and gives us food and drink, in her conduct she is Savitri and in her ideas Gayatri. She should not forget her importance. Unfortunately a number of movements for the empowerment of women protest against the atrocities inflicted on her but forget to remind her to be more responsible and live with dignity. She must extricate herself from the world of glamour, follow high ideas and draw inspiration from Sita, Gargi, Madalasa, Pannadhai and Mother Teresa, etc. If you ask any young woman in your family to name her role model, she would invariably come out with the name of some film personality. What can we expect of our new generation if they have such weaklings as their role model?

Such a society can never be conscious of its self-importance. Our women should project themselves as models. There is a competition between man and woman and the woman is clamouring for an equal status with man, but she has forgotten the ideal of our society which declares 'where women are respected, there reside the gods'. Say who is worshipped: the one who is equal the one who is superior to you? When man considers woman superior to himself why should she devalue herself by demanding an equal status with him? She needs introspect on this question. Someone has rightly pointed out that a woman is more important than a man because she has two more long vowels (i.e. a: after n and i: after r:) after the two consonants that form the word for man in Sanskrit. The words used for women show that she is ahead of man. What we need today is that women should wake up, make themselves an object of respect and not of sense gratification. A poet has rightly said:

No calamity will fall the world
The day women wake up
The flower of world peace will blossom
When mother's love rains on it.

What Others Say

1. With women, the heart argues, not the mind. – ***Matthew Arnold***
2. The prosperity and growing strength of a people ought to be attributed to their women. – ***Anonymous***
3. O fairest of creation! Last and best of all God's works. – ***John Milton***
4. O Woman! Lovely woman! Nature made thee to temper man, we had been brutes without you. – ***Thomas Otway***
5. The future of society is in the hands of mothers, if the world was lost through woman, she alone can save it. – ***Louis de Beaufort***
6. A handsome woman is a jewel, a good woman a treasure. – ***Saadi***
7. Men have sight, women insight. – ***Victor Hugo***
8. There will never be a generation of great men, until there has been a generation of free women and free mothers. – ***R.G. Inger Soll***
9. Women are never stronger than when they arm themselves with their weaknesses. – ***Madame Du Deffaud***
10. A perfect woman nobly planned
To warn, to comfort and command. – ***Wordsworth***

Laxmi

Life has no joy if we don't have any wealth but abundance of wealth also prompts us to immoral actions. It depends on man how he consecrates his wealth. One way to do so is to use it for acts of welfare. Goddess Laxmi never forsakes the person who dedicates his wealth to the service of mankind. She always supports him. Earning money is essential for leading a satisfactory life, but care should be taken about the means of earning it. Laxmi is the goddess of prosperity, wealth and money. No doubt money is so essential for us, but we should never give it over-importance or preference over other things. If we amass wealth by unjust means it does not do us any good. Only the money earned by just means without causing harm or exploiting others brings happiness to life and family.

Wealth is auspicious when procured by moral means and spent on charitable and welfare activities. Piety begets wealth, cleverness multiplies it, intelligence stabilizes it and restraint preserves it. The possession of wealth might not give as much joy as its loss gives pain. Wealth is a blessing for one who uses it to ameliorate the life of others.

Besides being affluent a man should also be intelligent. In the absence of intelligence wealth might bring about his decline and fall but with an intelligent person it increases. In this context it is said that one who is jealous and envious of others cannot keep hold of his wealth. It will soon depart and depute her elder sister poverty. Wealth dwells permanently in a house where there is peace and happiness. Some people are very greedy of money. They are ready to pick up a coin lying in muck. They are interested in money and not in the source from where it comes. They misapprehend that money can be earned only by dishonest means whereas the truth is just the reverse of it. The money earned by just and honest means is auspicious, gives peace and dwells with us for ever. It makes our home an abode of God whereas dishonesty invites poverty.

A truly rich person does not always think of money but grows generous with his growing wealth. The ungenerous and close fisted persons are really poor. A rich man should be kind and charitable. The wealth of an unmerciful person is like the money in the possession of a snake which is said to have a precious jewel in its head which is of no use to him. A liberal hearted person makes a beneficial use of his wealth.

The money earned by unjust and unrighteous means brings us dishonour and disgrace. The possession of wealth is not so important as the vision to use it purposefully. A person endowed with a benevolent point of view who knows how to utilize his wealth is a truly rich person. Society thanks and respects only such rich persons.

What Others Say

1. When wealth is neither enjoyed by oneself nor given to deserving persons the possessor becomes a disease to the society. ***– Kural***
2. The love of money is the root of all evil. ***– Bible***
3. It is easier to make money than to keep it. ***– Proverb***
4. Make all you can, save all you can, give all you can. ***– J. Wesley***
5. Dishonest money brings grief to all the family, but hating bribes brings happiness. ***– Bible***
6. Without a rich heart, wealth is a poor beggar. ***– Emerson***

7. Money should circulate like rain water.
– Thornton Wilder

8. There is nothing in the world so demoralizing as money. *– Sophocles*

9. I believe the power to make money is a gift of God.
– John D. Rockfeller

10. It is difficult for a rich man to be modest, or a modest person rich. *– Epictetus*

11. It is very difficult for the prosperous to be humble.
– Jone Austen

12. Money changes people just as often as it changes hands. *– Al Batt*

Friendship

A friend is one whom we cherish in our heart and who cherishes us in his, that is there is one soul in two bodies. Friendship is not just a relationship but a heart-felt deep experience. In our day-to-day life we come across a number of people who think and behave like us. We feel pleased in their company and freely exchange our thoughts and ideas with them. We share our pleasure and pain with them and cooperate with them. These persons are called our friends.

A true friend not only cooperates with us but also guides us to the path of progress. He may be relaxed and slack when we are happy but when we are in trouble he promptly comes to our help. The friendship which is free from selfishness, unreservedly frank and affably obliging lasts for the whole life-time and opens the gate of mutual progress. So be careful and awake when you fall into friendship with someone and then continue firm and constant. Never betray him.

Describing the qualities of a friend a wise men has said: He keeps his friend away from sin and turns him to work of welfare; keeps his secret concealed and exposes his noble qualities; does not forsake him in adversity and if needs be sacrifices for him all he has. He is like a lamp that shows us the path in darkness and leaves us as soon as the day light spreads, but we should not forget him who lighted our path. A poet regrets:

People forget those
Who keep them company in the dark
Who does not put out
The lamp as soon as the day dawns.

Friendship is a source of great experience, but unfortunately, at present it has become a show, a deception. Those who defile your character by their company never deserve to be your friends. A true friend is one who tenders advice for the welfare of all.

We often read about two persons joining together to commit a particular crime. An accomplice cannot be a friend for a true friend never drags you into the dark abyss of crime. This alliance breaks up as soon as their petty interest is served and they disappear like the horns of a hare.

Friendship is a touchstone that testifies your purity. About the friendship that degrades your character, an Urdu poet has said:

Were the enemies not hostile enough
That the friends have stepped forward.

Keep the friends who abet your evil tendencies at an arm's length. As a friend you should also take care to protect the character of your friend. The friendship based on virtuous qualities is best and everlasting.

What Others Say

1. Prosperity makes friends and adversity tries them. A true friend is one soul in two bodies. ***– Aristotle***
2. One friend in a life is much, two are many and three are hardly possible. ***– Henry Brooks Adams***
3. It is more shameful to distrust one's friends than to be deceived by them. ***– La Rochefoucauld***
4. Life is to be fortified by many friendships. To love, and to be loved, is the greatest happiness of existence. ***– Sydney Smith***
5. There are three faithful friends – an old wife, an old dog, and ready money. ***– Benjamin Franklin***
6. God, send me a friend that will tell me of my faults. ***– Thomas Fuller***

7. A faithful friend is a strong defence, and he that hath found such a one hath found a treasure. A faithful friend is the medicine of life. *– Bible*

8. Make friends who will force you to lever yourself up. *– Thomas J. Watson Sr.*

9. Friendships multiply joys and divide griefs.*– H. G. Bohn*

10. A true friend never gets in your way unless you happen to be going down. *– Arnold H. Glasow*

11. No man can be called friendless when he has God and the companionship of good books. *– Elizabeth Barrett Browning*

12. The best mirror is a friend's eye. *– Proverb*

13. A friend may well be reckoned the masterpiece of nature. *– R. W. Emerson*

Offspring

Offspring is the most charming outcome of conjugal relationship. It fills the married life with cheerful bustling activity and merriment. A person blessed with children is considered lucky and his life happy and auspicious if the children turn out to be well-mannered. If the children have good qualities, are wise and willing to serve others they make life all the more cheerful, and contented, otherwise the parent's life becomes a hell. They face a dilemma; they can neither drive the children away nor reform them easily. They are doomed to a life of frustration, vexation and depression. It is not enough to have children we should raise them properly, provide them good education and training and sympathize with their feelings. It is rather more important. On the other hand the children are also expected to come true to the expectations of the parents and behave in socially approved ways.

If the parents fail to do their duty, they will do no good to their family, community and the country. People today make all efforts to provide every facility to their children but neglect to impart them good manners. Why do they commit this sin of omission when they give so much time and attention to earning money which they amass only to bequeath them? For a proper development and upbringing of children we should double the time we devote them now and reduce the expenses on them by one half because they will requite to the society with what they have seen and learnt at home.

For this the parents should themselves first cultivate good manners to be able to present good models before the children and infuse and inspire them to fulfil their duties. Indian culture equates parents with gods, so they should themselves develop divine qualities to impart to the children. They should themselves lead an ideal life. And because the parents are the first teachers of children it is their bounden duty to do so.

For a proper care of our children, our culture has divided their development into various stages; fondly love them till they are five years of age. Chastise them till they reach the tenth year of their age. And when they attain the age of sixteen a father should treat his son and the mother her daughter as their friend. Don't impose too strict a discipline on them nor give them unrestrained freedom. Let the atmosphere in the home be civilized, noble and peaceful because it is the home where the children learn the first lesson in socialization. A loving and congenial atmosphere, holy and pure food and life style exert a divine influence on the children. On the other hand if the atmosphere is vitiated by strife, disaffection and impiety it will be hellish. Children raised in an atmosphere of goodwill and peaces serve their old parents voluntarily.

What Others Say

1. Every child comes with the message that God is not yet discouraged of man. – ***Rabindranath Tagore***
2. If you cannot hold children in your arms, please hold them in your hearts. – ***Mother Clara Hale***
3. Men are more careful of the breed of their horses and dogs than of their children. – ***Penn***
4. Children are the anchors that hold a mother to life. – ***Sophocles***
5. There is no finer investment for any community than putting milk into babies. – ***Winston Churchill***
6. Children have more need of models than of critics. – ***Joseph and Soubert***

7. To make your children capable of honesty is the beginning of education. – ***John Ruskin***

8. Next to God, thy parents. – ***Penn***

9. Of all nature's gifts to the human race, what is sweeter to a man than his children? – ***John Ray***

10. A wise son maketh a glad father. – ***Proverb***

11. Train up a child in the way he should go and when he is old, he will not depart from it. – ***Proverb***

12. What's done to children, they will do to society. – ***Karl Menninger***

13. The hardest job kids face today is learning good manners without seeing any. – ***Fred Astaire***

14. Parents can give everything but common sense. – ***Proverb***

15. The best inheritance a parent can give his children is a few minutes to his time each day. – ***O.A. Battista***

Generation Gap

There has always been a gap between the generations, but it did not cause so many problems as it has created today. The problems have not only become more complicated but given rise to conflict. Now the people belonging to two or three generations find it difficult to live amicably under one roof. Is this conflict inevitable or can it be averted?

When members belonging to different generations live together conflict of interests and ideas between them is very likely to occur. Tiffs are common in family and social relations. But if the members of the older generation try to understand the feelings of the young generation and mould themselves accordingly the rift between them may be bridged smoothly.

There was a time when the family and social relationships were considered venerable and great care was taken to maintain them. We believed in the ideal of a world family so had the joint family system in which the members of three or four generations lived together under a roof. But gradually the joint family disintegrated and the nuclear family replaced it.

Once philanthropy was considered a virtue but today an individual prefers his selfish interest to that of all others. Father and son, brothers and sisters, and husbands and wives have knocked the door of the court to demand division of their property and wealth. The feeling of sacrifice is dying up gradually. Earlier the people subscribed to the ideal of simple living and high thinking, but now the values have changed. People are carried away by the glamour of the materialistic world. Ideas have outlived their importance and everyone runs after luxury. Fashions, people's choices, habits and dresses all have changed with the passage of time. Once women detested the world of glamour and even female role in films were played by men. Later on when women actresses entered the theatre they were fully covered from top to bottom but today they have stripped themselves off and only the one who has almost bared her body is popular.

The old generations do not approve the ways of the present generation because their thinking is 25, 50 or 75 years behind time and they have yet failed to come out of their times and this has been the chief cause of conflict between the generations. They want the new generation to live in their way and invite trouble. However, the young generation is also to blame. Born in the computer age it has access to greater information and considers the older generation outmoded and incompetent. Hence, it is unwilling to take even a useful advice from it and there is always a point of clash. No doubt everything is subject to change but relations are an exception. A father remains a father whatever be the way of his thinking.

Two or three generations have always existed together in every society. If they are well-adjusted and have developed a mutual understanding, there is no reason why this gap between them lead to a conflict. But no adjustment between them is possible unless the older generation understands the young generation and moulds itself accordingly. It must move with the times and modify its thinking and instead of domineering over the young generation have friendly terms with it. The new generation should also learn how to develop amicable terms with them instead of conflict. There is no doubt that the older generation is a treasure house of knowledge and experience and whatever it says is for the good of the young people.

The old and the new generations should live together and help each other in times of need. They must be sensitive to each other.

Difference on a point should not be made a question of ego but sorted out good-humouredly. When faced with an adverse situation the two should put their heads together to devise a strategy to get out of it.

The problem of generation gap is age-old and needs concerted efforts on both the sides to solve it. They must compromise with each other and the young generation should pay its respects to the older one.

What Others Say

1. Every generation revolts against its fathers and makes friends with its grandfathers. *– Lewis Mumford*

Learning

In Hindu mythology Vidya (learning) is the goddess of knowledge. It is our third eye. The two physical eyes give us information about the outer world but Vidya reveals the internal world. Without the knowledge of the inner self, the knowledge of outer world is incomplete. It means we are still ignorant.

Vidya literally means to know. Whatever we learn is 'Vidya' or learning. As the sphere of knowledge and learning expands our information becomes deeper. Learning is a perennial process that continues for the whole life. It is the result of manipulating all the available resources in a particular area. Education is essential for life; it is the right of man.

Learning is an invaluable treasure, an adornment of life and a symbol of humanity. It is the most precious wealth and imparting knowledge is the greatest charity. A learned man is honoured everywhere and in all circumstances. Everyone should try to acquire knowledge that makes him wise and cultured, expends his thinking, empowers him to resist orthodoxy and enables him to get rid of it.

Learning is a strange, incomparable and unique means that leads man from darkness to light, from falsehood to truth and from death to immortality. It makes him a man in the true sense and lays the foundation of a progressive society.

Knowledge is the best possession for us in the world. No one can steal it nor does it diminish with distribution. A man can acquire wisdom by slowly studying the relevant texts. Knowledge makes us modest which sharpens our ability. In its turn ability brings in wealth and paves our way to righteousness and peace. The man who makes a practical use of his learning and knowledge is better man dozens who roam in the world of imagination and theory only. It is a secret wealth which acts as Kamdhenu (a cow that yields all one desires) in times of adversity and as a mother in a foreign land. So he must make all effort to acquire.

When you sit to study, sit as a famished person with a vigorous desire to eat but digest well whatever you eat. One who fails to do so is unable to ruminate over it at leisure. A learned person who does not put his learning to practical use in life is like a beast of burden with a load of books. Even when enjoying perfect happiness, a man should not overlook the utility of learning.

A thinker says learning has no meaning for one who loves pleasure and for a student pleasure is useless. So one who hankers after pleasure should not hope to gain knowledge. The success of an institution, a business, an organization or a country depends on its members and their attitude. By introducing change in his attitude and behaviour, a man can improve his life.

To elevate our society and country we need people with strong character who are honest and endowed with a positive and ethical point of view in whatever field they might happen to work. The educated persons always work with courage and intelligence in all circumstances. The mark of a truly educated person is that he is able to distinguish between intelligence and foolishness, good and evil, decent and indecent whether he possesses a university degree or not.

What Others Say

1. He who adds not to his learning, diminishes it.
   – The Talmud

2. We should not ask who is the most learned, but who is the best learned. ***– Montaigne***

3. He who learns, and makes no use of his learning, is a beast of burden with a load of books. – ***Saadi***
4. All want to be learned, but no one is willing to pay the price. – ***Juvenal***
5. Learning is not child's play, we cannot learn without pain. – ***Aristotle***
6. The love of money and the love of learning rarely meet. – ***George Herbert***
7. Seeing much, suffering much and studying much, are the three pillars of learning. – ***Benjamin Franklin***
8. Much learning shows how little mortals know.
9. A learned man has always wealth in himself. – ***Latin Proverb***
10. They know enough who know how to learn. – ***Henry Brooks Adams***
11. The foundation of every state is the education of its youth. – ***Diogenes***
12. The direction in which education starts a man will determine his future life. – ***Plato***
13. Education has for its object the formation of character. – ***Herbert Spencer***
14. Learning without thinking is useless. Thinking without learning is dangerous. – ***Confucius***
15. He who has inagination without learning has wings but no feet. – ***Joseph Jaubert***
16. Learning sleeps and snores in libraries, but wisdom is everywhere, wide awake, on tiptoe. – ***Josh Billings***
17. Learning is not attained by chance. It must he sought for with ardour and attended with diligence. – ***Abigail Adams***
18. The library is the temple of learning, and learning has liberaed more people than all the wars in history. – ***Carl Rowan.***

Business

The Sanskrit word for business literally means behaviour and it is behaviour concerned with a particular work involving economic transaction with a view to earning profit. A true and just business aims at earning a reasonable profit without causing any loss to others. To lead his life and to raise his family a man needs some source of income and for this some take to service and some to business. For business one should be familiar with its nature besides being honest, industrious, devout and self-confident.

We should not aim at making an easy profit. It is praiseworthy to earn money by righteous and just means, for if it is earned illegally or by exploiting others it gives only a temporary pleasure, but no satisfaction. Business activities affect our character and the welfare of our family so money should be earned and spent honestly and auspiciously

A successful businessman has the same relation with his customer as the bee has with a flower. She sucks its sap but does not damage it so that she may continue to get it in future also. We should be upright in our business or our life will be inglorious. The business based on fraudulent and deceitful practices is soon cut short. So a businessman should carry out his business as a religious ceremony and treat his business establishment holier than a temple. A true and gentle businessman maintains an even balance between money and righteousness. He must be absolutely honest in his dealings or it will be a theft and a deceitful activity. If the profit, though modest, brings in satisfaction our business is on holy lines, but if we feel greedy, it means we are drifting away from high ideals.

I am reminded of an incident in the life of a devout businessman. A country had to face a fierce famine. People began to die in large numbers. One night, the king had a dream that if an honest person prayed it might rain. A businessman Tuladhar by name touched his balance in the presence of a number of people and said, 'If I have earned profit without ever harming anyone, let God listen to my prayer.' And lo! It began to rain profusely; the crops revived and peace and prosperity returned. The prayer of one honest businessman performed the miracle to the surprise of all.

Such business is benevolent to us as well as to others. It is said that when the sounds of holy prayers offered in a temple reach your business establishment, your wealth grows and paves way for everything auspicious in life.

What Others Say

1. The art of winning in business is in working hard not taking things so seriously. – ***Elbert Hubbard***
2. I do not believe you can do today's job with yesterday's methods and be in business tomorrow. – ***Nelson Jackson***
3. Business first : pleasure afterwards. – ***Thackeray***
4. Buying and selling is essentially antisocial. – ***Edward Bellamy***
5. Few people do business well who do nothing else. – ***Earl of Chesterfield***
6. Trade is a social act. – ***John Stuart Mill***
7. The customer is always right. – ***H.G. Selfridge***
8. When you are skinning your customers you should leave some skin on to grow again so that you can skin them again. – ***Nikita Khrushchev***

9. Whenever you see a successful businessman, someone once made a courageous decision. *– Peter Drucker*

10. In the end, all business operations can be reduced to three words: people, product, and profits. People come first. *– Lee Iacocca*

11. It either is or ought to be evident to every one that business has to prosper before anybody can get any benefit from it. *– Theodore Roosevelt*

12. Business is like riding a bicycle. Either you keep moving or you fall down. *– John David Wright*

13. To a man of business, talk business, go to your business and leave him to his business. *– Anonymous*

14. If you wish something done, ask a busy man to do it. *– Anonymous*

Income

A person's income is what he earns by virtue of his talent, industry and luck. Everyone in the world wants to grow rich quickly so very often he adopts injust means to earn money. A robber may become rich by robbing others, but he cannot use this money in socially acceptable way nor cannot he earn respect in the society.

Only the money earned as a result of honesty, industry and devotion can be termed valid income. Money acquires divinity if it is used for charitable purposes. It grows hundred-fold by the grace of God and brings in joy, satisfaction and prosperity and develops right attitude. Considering money essential for life, some people blindly run after it. They might grow rich but fail to enjoy life.

Wealth may be used for charity or consumption or it may simply be squandered. If a person neither consumes his wealth nor does he give it in charity it is sure to go to waste. Consider some of the sayings of Shruti. Wealth enhances the prestige of your family. It makes you charitable but excess of wealth is a curse. Too much importance given to money in the present day world has turned everything topsy-turvy. Remember, money acts either as a servant or a master. It has been rightly said that the rich who are burning in the fire of greed long for money all the more. The truly rich is one who spends within his means. It has rightly been said that if you can live within your means you must have got a money-generating magic wand. Wealth like manure is not of much use unless well-spread out. Money is called liquid that is it must always circulate otherwise like stagnant water it begins to stink.

Wealth behaves in a strange way. The one who has it feels as if he were flying in the sky and the one who renounces it feels fuddled with ego. The one who desires to win praise by renouncing it declares his addiction to it. The one who consumes it is not much different from the one who renounces it. The consumer grips it while the renouncer releases it but both value it in their heart. The consumer is greedy so he runs after wealth and the renounces is afraid of it and runs away from it. There is nothing intrinsic in wealth that one should either grip it or release it.

We can make an auspicious use of wealth by spending it for charitable purposes. The growth of wealth should bring in more prosperity. And if it does not, there is something wrong in your thinking. It is not a healthy outlook if you think that your wealth must be used for your family and your friends alone.

Wealth should be used for philanthropy because thus one can get salvation with one hundredth of the efforts the fools make to earn wealth. Those who give too much importance to wealth hardly see the difference between the rich and the poor. Abstaining from food for a day and from water for an hour puts both on the same level. No doubt money is useful for life in this world yet it is not all in all. Learn the art of earning money but before that learn the art of spending it properly or it may push you on the path of evil.

Changing values of life have made man ravenous for money. Those who wish to amass wealth by hook or by crook should know that it comes from noble deeds only. The money earned by foul means lasts at the most for ten years and as soon as the eleventh year begins it takes wing. Day in and day out we read in newspapers and watch on news channels that the hoarded black money is either confiscated by the government raids or carried away by thieves and robbers. The man who hopes to get rid of his pain and suffering should never forget that he can not get relief with the money squeezed out of others.

It is a matter of general observation that the ill-begotten money is used for footing hospital bills or indulging in criminal and inauspicious activities which end in ruin and disgrace. Those who wish to earn merit by spending money should develop an attitude of self-denial and sacrifice and look upon their wealth as public property to be used for public welfare. Only such persons are truly rich.

What Others Say

1. The love of someone else's money is the root of all evil.
2. When money speaks the truth is silent.

   – Russian Proverb
3. The darkest hour of any man's life is when he sits down to plan how to get money without earning it.

   – Horace Greeley
4. A fool and his money are soon parted.
5. A fool may make money, but it needs a wise man to spend it.
6. Money is a good servant but a bad master.
7. It is easier to make money than to keep it.

   – Yiddish Proverb
8. Income is something you can't live without or within.
9. Income always looks bigger coming than going.
10. I don't live within my income because I can't afford it.
11. Money is like an arm or leg : use it or lose it.

    – Henry Ford
12. Nothing hurts worse than the loss of money. *– Livy*
13. He must have killed a lot of people to have gotten so rich. *– Moliere*
14. The rich have many consolations. *– Plato*
15. I believe the power to make money is a gift of God.

    – John D. Rockefeller
16. You cannot keep out of trouble by spending more than your income. *– William J.H. Booteker*

Borrowing

There are some who have described borrowing as the most fatal disease whereas others have recommended it for the enjoyment of life. Only he knows the burden of borrowing who bears it on his shoulders. Those who seem to enjoy it are not aware of the pain they shall feel when repaying it with interest. The payment of interest on a loan is perhaps the most painful experience for the borrower.

Borrowing means taking money or some other thing from someone on promise of redeeming it at a later date. Indian culture speaks of three debts – the one we owe to divines, the one we owe to the rishis and the one we owe to our parents. A person tries to repay them all by performing auspicious acts in his life time.

Under the impact of consumerism these days we are living in a loan culture. We should restrain our wants and make do with whatever we earn without borrowing from others. Shruti says, 'One who goes to borrow invites trouble for himself.' If the loan is small the borrower feels indebted to you but if it is large he becomes your enemy. The father who dies without repaying his loan is the greatest enemy of his children.

Debt is a noose that deviously strangulates the debtor. It is an obstinate guest that never leaves your home once it has entered it.

Never leave a debt unliquidated, a fire unextinguished and a disease partly cured for they would soon erupt to big dimensions. Unfortunately the prevalence of loan culture these days has spurred the spirit of competition among men. They are freely contracting loans for housing and vehicles, etc. but the monthly instalments they have to pay have divided them into as many pieces. In the days gone by a man tried to live within his means but today his average expenditure often outdoes it. Availability of everything on instalments has now made man a slave to material comforts.

Man has become lazy today. He loves luxuries and hates labour. He must avoid acting on the maxim 'Borrow and enjoy' for excessive love for physical facilities and pleasure permanently cripples a man. Outstanding debt not only tells upon our economy but also on our physical and mental health. Desist from borrowing lest the pressure of paying instalments should shorten your life span.

What Others Say

1. Neither a borrower nor a lender be;
   for loan oft loses both itself and friend.
   And borrowing dulls the edge of husbandry.
   – ***Shakespeare***
2. Who goeth a borrowing goeth a sorrowing. – ***Tusser.***
3. A creditor is worse than a mater; for a master owns only your person, a creditor owns your dignity, and can be- labour that. – ***Victor Hugo***
4. Borrowing is not much better than begging. – ***German Proverb***
5. Borrowing the mother of trouble. – ***Hebrew Proverb***
6. He who does not have to borrow lives without cares. – ***Yiddish Proverb***
7. Debt is the slavery of the free. – ***Publilius Syrus***
8. Debt is the worst poverty. – ***M. G. Lichtwer***
9. Debts shorten life. – ***Joseph Joubert***
10. There can be no freedom or beauty about a home life that depends on borrowing and debt. – ***Henrik Ibsen***

Books

If you wish to know a person, find out who his friends are and what books he reads. Books are a true index of a person's character. A right-minded person would go in for good books. The world of a book lover is his own; he is always happy wherever he might be. Books can change the direction of our life, they can agitate our feelings and cause a revolution. Good literature is as important as a good physician. Good books shower happiness on us and make our soul noble. Like good friends they mould our personality.

A thinker says, 'I shall welcome books even in hell because they can turn any place into heaven.' The wisdom collected and enshrined in books is more valuable than precious stones which glitter in the world outside whereas the books enlighten our inner self. They fill the mind with the fragrance of righteous ideas and have been rightly compared to a garden carried in the pocket. The glory and greatness of human culture is contained within the covers of books.

All the thoughts, deeds and achievements of the human race are preserved in the enchanting pages of books. Through them we can simultaneously live the experiences of several generations. They provide a beautiful bridge across time. They connect the present with the past and direct us to a bright future. Look what a book lover says: Books and the memory of my beloved never let me feel lonely anywhere. They are my true companions. In fact, man has no better friend than books. The ocean enclosed between their covers contains a lot of pearls and gems. A poet has rightly said:

Books are a storehouse of knowledge
They are the basis of our life,
Like a strong puff of wind
They change the course of our life.

The man who compresses the most of his knowledge within the shortest space is the best writer, but better than him is the reader who preserves that auspicious knowledge within his heart and expresses it into his conduct. Hitopadesh divides knowledge into two classes the knowledge of arms and the knowledge of scriptures. The art of weaponry declines, for the veteran warrior is unable to practise it in his old age, but the knowledge of scriptures thrives all the more with advancing years. It is true that the world cherishes the memory of a person who has written something worth reading or done something worth writing about. We should cultivate the habit of self study, for it is the books alone that teach us the best way of living a life.

What Others Say

1. A good book is the precious life blood of a master spirit, embalmed and treasured up on purpose to a life beyond life. ***– Milton***
2. Next to acquiring good friends, the best acquisition is that of good books. ***– Colton***
3. A good book contains more real wealth than a good bank. ***– Roy & Smith***
4. Books are the quietest and most constant friends; they are the most accessible and wisest of counsellors, and the most patient teachers. ***– Charles W. Eliot***
5. A room without books is like a body without a soul. ***– Cicero***
6. It is from books that wise men desire consolation in the troubles of life. ***– Victor Hugo***

7. Friends, books, a cheerful heart, and conscience clear are the most choice companions we have here.
– William Mather

8. A book is like a garden carried in the pocket.
– Chinese Proverb

9. Books are the treasured wealth of the world and the fit inheritance of generations and nations.
– Henry David Thoreau

10. Books are for nothing but to inspire. *– R.W. Emerson*

11. The proper study of mankind is books.
– Aldous Leonard Huxley

12. Books without the knowledge of life are useless.
– Samnel Johnson

13. No man can be called friendless when he has God and the companionship of good books.
– Elizabeth Barrett Browning

14. Books support us in our solitude and keep us from being a burden to ourselves. *– Jeremy Collier*

15. A great book should leave you with many experiences and slightly exhausted at the end you live several lives while reading it. *– William Styron*

16. Tell we what you read and I'll tell you who you are.
– Francois Mauriac

Body

Man's body is an abode of God. To make it a temple and our heart a shrine we should perform all righteous deeds and establish godliness in our body. The scriptures tell us that our body is meant for performing charitable deeds and should be used for that purpose alone because we get it after having passed through a number of bodies. We should maintain carefully good physical and mental health. The importance of body lies in performing both secular and sacred deeds. We can work well and worship God only when our body is fit. Body is perishable but the deeds performed through it are everlasting. We should be regular and moderate in our food habits to lead a healthy life.

Health is the greatest wealth and we get an ailment free body by the grace of God. Body, not being important in itself need not be pampered; it is simply a means to ensure the well-being of our spirit. A healthy body and a cheerful heart indicate our outer and inner wellbeing. Our health depends on the daily regimen we follow. Simple and nutritious diet and a disciplined life style are a key to healthy life. We should look after both our body and health. We shall never fall ill if we rise and go to bed and take our meals and exercises at fixed hours.

In this age of competition we all aim at securing a handsome income but it should not be at the cost of our health because a disease free body is the first requisite for happiness. To keep our body fit we should follow a regular routine of drinking water in the morning, milk at bed time and butter milk with lunch. Good health and good understanding are the two blessings for life. You can earn money by sacrificing your health, but you cannot recover it by spending money. If we maintain a healthy body we can hope to live a hundred years.

If we depart this life before completing our tenure it will be an insult to God because he bestowed this human body on us to perform virtuous acts and not just to earn money. Experienced persons advise us to carry out planned works of welfare while we are free from diseases for we do not know when death might knock at our door and cut us off from doing noble deeds. Our body being an abode of God is as pure and sacred as a place of pilgrimage. We should not defile it with ominous conduct and deeds. A healthy body is a guesthouse for the soul whereas an unhealthy one is a prison house.

Spiritual thinking considers body and soul as two distinct entities. The soul departs leaving the body here. Childhood and old age are the stages of body and not of soul which is part of the imperishable Supreme Being and gives up this body at the appointed time. You are master of your body and must keep it fit because you are rewarded for actions performed by you through the agency of your body.

Body has been compared to a boat and the soul to a sailor. If the boat is strong and the sailor well and wakeful we can cross the ocean of this world. If the sailor is cautions and careful he will safely take us to the shore. But if the boat is dilapidated and worn out, howsoever skilled and wakeful the sailor might be, he cannot save us from drowning into the whirlpool. Hence to successfully accomplish this journey of life, we should have a healthy body together with guiltless mind and ideas and untainted spirit and consciousness.

What Others Say

1. The body says what words cannot. – ***Martha Graham***

2. Your body is the temple of the Holy Ghost, which is in you, which ye have of God, and ye are not your own.
   – ***Bible***

3. From a man's face, I can read his character, if I can see him walk, I know his thoughts. – ***Petronius***

4. If anything is sacred, the human body is sacred. – ***Walt Whitman***

5. No one is free who is a slave to the body. – ***L.A. Seneca***

6. It is a great fortune to get the human body. – ***Anonymous***

Food

Eating, sleeping, defending and copulating are the natural propensities of all living creatures. In the language of psychology they are called instincts. Hunger is associated with food; when we need food we feel hungry. When the measure of food once taken is digested we feel hungry again. Man is ready to do anything to satisfy his hunger, he does not hesitate to commit even the gravest crime. Hunger develops as well as destroys relations and can turn a man into a demon. Let us understand what is hunger, analyze it and then try to satisfy it.

Besides physical hunger, stimulate your mental hunger too and try to satisfy it by studying good literature, mixing with gentle people or reciting hymns in praise of God. Never let physical hunger overpower you or else it would destroy everything. The food we eat must he auspicious; it must satisfy hunger but not arouse our evil tendencies. Pure and seasonable food provides nutrition to our body and generates noble thoughts in our mind. Let us pursue the maxim 'Eat to live and not live to eat'. Our thoughts and actions are shaped by the food we partake. Hence, we must be careful about both hunger and food.

Moreover we should not care only to satisfy our own hunger, for it is said that a charitable person who feeds others wields greater power than a selfish saint. Hunger is a poignant experience: a hungry woman casts away her own son and a hungry serpent eats her own eggs. Hunger is all pervasive. Like any other person, the cripple lying on the footpath also needs food. Hence efforts should be made to feed him too.

Food must be healthful, amenable and restrained that is we need a nutritious, palatable and balanced diet to sustain our body. An imbalanced diet might cause indigestion and other ailments that gradually drag a person towards his death. We should eat only good food and not whatever we fancy.

Hunger is closely associated with hard work and it is often seen that the rich have a poor appetite whereas the poor can digest all they eat. Food forms part of our culture too. We respectfully offer food to our guests and politely entreat them to take more and more of the meals. Commenting on this custom someone has remarked that we continue to serve till the diner says 'no' or shakes his little finger to refuse and stop only when he grunts a roar.

The next question that we face is what we should eat and how much, for even the animals are aware of it. A man should not eat only to satisfy his taste buds. His food should be hygienic and nourishing to his body and mind. Simple and wholesome food generates gentle and pious ideas whereas impure and contaminated food pollutes our conduct.

Over the centuries, our tradition has asserted that food shapes our ideas and water, our speech. If we take a balanced diet as a gift of God it fills us with unprecedented joy and enthusiasm. Those who succumb to taste are slaves of the senses and are advised to change their disposition.

All religious texts lay great emphasis on exercising restraint in matters of food habits. Hinduism, Jainism and Buddhism prescribe a number of fasts for this purpose. Islam and Christianity also insist on fasting. Be careful about your food habits if you wish to have a healthy body, mind and soul.

What Others Say

1. Man is what he eats. ***– Ludwig Andreas Fenerbach***
2. A hungry man is not a free man. ***– Adlai Stevenson***

3. If you wish to grow thinner, diminish your dinner.
– H.S. Leigh

4. The destiny of contries depends on the way they feed themselves. *– Anthelme Brittat-Savarigh*

5. Tell me what you eat, and I will tell you what you are.
– Ibid

6. One cannot think well, love well, sleep well, if one has not dined well. *– Virginia Woolf*

7. There is no love sincerer than the love of food.
– Bernard Shaw

8. Whatever will satisfy hunger is good food.
– Chinese Proverb

9. Never eat more than you can lift.

Youth

Youth is the period of spring in human life and as flowers blossom everywhere in this season with bees humming round them, the flowers of new energy, new zeal and new joy appear in a young person and the bees of fanciful dreams and aspirations begin to cluster round them. Those who are desirous of leaving the mark of their success on the sand of time are truly young.

The period of youth begins after adolescence and is the third stage in human development. When you are between the age of twenty and thirty, have a spirit bubbling with enthusiasm and a body bursting with energy and lead a care-free life, it means that you are young. The youth fearlessly soar high up in the sky of hope and are ever ready to measure the whole earth with their steps. They have an exuberance of creativity and an indomitable courage to confront any one in the world.

Youth is a violent storm too difficult to control and subdue. The moralists hold that anyone endowed with youth, wealth, authority or impudence is a threat to the society and the one who possesses all these four is a veritable challenge to peace. The youthful mind is always willing to learn new things and is free from the misapprehension that everything worth knowing in the world has already been known. He never grows old and decrepit in his disposition and is ever ready to change and transform himself. The youth is capable of giving a new turn to the wheels of time. No doubt the youth is passionate and impetuous, but if it is equipped with the eyes of discretion and sagacity it may set a powerful revolution in motion.

Every revolution be it social, political or spiritual in a society, nation or the world has been initiated by the youth. The vigour and ardour of the youth and their resolution to sacrifice their life may always be discerned at the back of a battle-field, a scientific laboratory and a movement for social change or even for a country's freedom. The bulwark of a country whose youth are deficient in the strength of their body, mind and character is fragile and a person, a caste, a community or a nation resting against a drooping prop cannot survive long.

To protect and preserve the youth of the nation our policy makers must direct the youth power in positive channels. The youth have already set records in the field of science, arts, sports and literature and deserve to be put at the helm of the country's affairs. If the zeal of the youth combines with the experience of the elders, it can change the shape of the country.

Often, the people complain that the country's youth have gone astray, but this is one sided opinion because it applies to the guides of the country in equal measure. When the leadership has deviated from the right path how can it hope the youth to follow it. We must dismiss this negative assessment of the youth. Make the youth a harbinger of change and place the burden of responsibility on their shoulders and they shall automatically take to nobility, patience and serenity. Let the youth record the story of their virility, faith, passion and energy on the pages of history. Help them consolidate their aspirations and resolutions and then see how they change the destiny of the country.

What Others Say

1. Everybody's youth is a dream, a form of chemical madness. – ***Scott Fitzgerald***
2. There is a feeling of eternity in youth, to be young is to be one of the immortal gods. – ***William Hazlitt***

3. Almost everything that is great has been done by youth. – ***Benjamin Disraeli***
4. The days of our youth are the days of our glory. – ***Lord Byron***
5. The young are permanently in a state resembling intoxication, for youth is sweet and they are growing. – ***Aristotle***
6. Youth is like spring, an over praised season. – ***Samuel Butler***
7. Pay attention to the young, and make them just as good as possible. – ***Socrates***
8. Youth is unending intoxication, it is a fever of the mind. – ***La Rochefoucauld***
9. The denunciation of the young is a necessary part of the hygiene of older people, and greatly assists the circulation of the blood. – ***Logan Pearsall Smith***
10. It is easier to have the vigour of youth when you are old than the wisdom of age when you are young. – ***Richard J. Needham***
11. The secret of staying young is to live honestly, eat slowly and just not think about your age. – ***Lucille Ball***
12. You will stay young as long as you learn, from new habits and don't mind being contradicted. – ***Marie Von Ebner - Eschenbach***
13. You are young at any age if you are planning for tomorrow.
14. The young do not know enough to be prudent and therefore they attempt the impossible and achieve it, generation after generation. – ***Pearl S. Buck.***

Old Age

Old Age is the evening of life. Both the morning and the evening have their own specific beauty and charm. To make the leisure hours of the evening joyful and pleasing man must modify his outlook that an old man is a tired, inactive and motionless person. Old age simply means that a person has advanced in years and has consequently developed and matured. If we have a positive outlook, old age will appear a blessing but if we have a negative one it will seem a curse. To make the old age a blessing, one should:

(i) Make this fourth stage of life i.e. old age a period of hope, for ill-health, despondence and physical debility make old age burdensome.

(ii) Refrain from unnecessarily interfering in others' affairs. Have faith in new generation and advise it when necessary.

(iii) Somehow keep oneself active. To do so and remain associated with social progress one should spend a lot of his time in social service or some other useful activities.

(iv) Feel as much happy to see the youth, assimilate some of their qualities, as they feel when they see an old person enlivened with the qualities of the youth.

One who believes in the above maxims may grow old physically and not mentally, for a truly old person is one who depends on others and has lost his zeal and virility. An active person never grows old. Spend your youth in a way that you don't have to repent in your old age.

Old age is a storehouse of experiences and an old man is the biggest school on the earth. He may have a shaking neck, a wrinkled face and tottering legs but in his feelings and actions his decrepit body reflects the flow of resolution. To make his old age worthwhile, one should drive away the mentality of withdrawal from the world. Instead of drowning himself into the dark abyss of despondence he should keep the flame of meditation and consciousness burning and make old age a challenge to the world instead of just waiting for it to end.

Instead of treating old age as a waiting room for death treat it as a natural destination of the journey of life. During youth you remained involved in worldly activities, observed customs and rituals, discharged your duties and responsibilities as also enjoyed the pleasures of the world, now during the old age conserve and enrich your spiritual energy. Simply performing rites and rituals or singing hymns in a temple does not make one spiritual. Spiritualism means that you wholehearted surrender your consciousness at the feet of the Supreme Consciousness that is God. True spiritualism consists in instilling hope in the heart of those whose eyes are suffused and for this we should follow proper rules of conduct, service and philanthropy.

For a proper utilization of your old age cultivate the habit of self-study. Instead of whiling away your time in idle gossiping and wasteful activities, read good literature, for it guides the youth and makes old age serene, graceful and comfortable. If you have the creative ability, write your reminiscences when you are nearing the close of your life. They might serve as a beacon light for the new generation. Consider old age not a burden but a source of new energy. Follow a simple and active routine of life and experience a new fountain of energy springing in you.

What Others Say

1. When grace is joined with wrinkles, it is adorable. There is an unspeakable dawn in happy old age.
   – Victor Hugo

2. You will stay young as long as you learn, form new habits and don't mind being contradicted.
   – Marie Von Ebner Eschenbach

3. To age with dignity and with courage cuts close to what it is to be a man. ***– Roger Kahn***

4. Old age is when you know all the answers but nobody asks you the questions.

5. You know you are getting old when you've got money to burn, but the fires gone out. ***– Hy Gardner***

6. Old age has its pleasures, which though different, are not less than the pleasures of youth.
   – W.Somerset Maugham

7. There are so few who can grow old with a good grace.
   – Richard Steele

8. To know how to grow old is the master work of wisdom, and one of the most difficult chapters in the art of living.
   – Amiel

9. One's last years are like the final chapter of a very exciting movel. ***– Lionel Curtistos***

Death

Describing death a poet points out the transience of human life saying:

What about life on earth
Pearly drops on flowers and hope in tears!

Death is inevitable. One who is born on this earth is sure to die, and when it is the destiny of all why to fear it? God has also prescribed the way one shall die. But life does not consist just in taking birth and passing away. We may seek self-satisfaction in death but for the world it remains a tragedy. With his noble qualities such as liberality, kindness, philanthropy and sensitivity as also devotion to God, a person can make even his death a memorable event. One who is steeped in devotion to God, has subdued his senses by restraining his mind, will meet his death fearlessly.

Death is not a terror, but a sound sleep followed by cheerful reawakening. It is the golden key that can unlock the door of immortality. It is not a curse but a blessing because God takes back what he had given you and you must be thankful to him for redeeming your debt. Death is the greatest adventure in life and a poet jokes about it.

I'll behave rudely, but once in my life
Friends will walk on foot, and I ride up their shoulders.
Death strengthens and not weakens a man for
Who could not rise from bed until yesterday
Became strong enough today to depart the world.

Look at another funny couplet that celebrates death

Once people stood up to honour me
But today they are sitting to bid me good bye.

We make preparations before undertaking a job. Similarly, we must prepare ourselves to meet death while we are still alive. We should never let the idea of death slip from our mind even for a moment and brace ourselves by recounting the name of God. It will resolve the mystery of death. Death is the final guest that calls at our door, hence it deserves a respectful welcome. Greet him with joy, but if you start crying and bewailing at his sight, it is a disgrace to him. If we cheerfully greet death and praise it, it becomes a celebration. Life and death are the two sides of the same coin. One who sees life in death and never forgets it is a true man of action and lives the life of a sincere Yogi.

What Others Say

1. Dying is an art, like everything else. – ***Sylvia Plath***
2. No man should be afraid to die, who hath under stood what it is to live. – ***Thomas Fuller***
3. He that lives to forever, never fears dying. – ***William Penn***
4. Men fear death as children fear to go in the dark. – ***Francis Bacon***
5. Death is the crown of life. Were death denied, poor man would live in vain to live, would not be life. Even fools would be wise to die. – ***Edward Young***
6. Death is certain for the born and rebirth inevitable for the dead. You should not grieve over the inevitable. – ***Bhagvad Gita***
7. The true tomb of the dead is the heart of the living. – ***Jean Cocteau***
8. You don't get to choose how you're going to die. Or, when. You can only decide how you're going to live. Now. – ***Joan Balz***
9. The only religious way to think of death is as part and parcel of life. – ***Thomas Mann***
10. There is no death. Only a change of worlds. – ***Seattle***
11. Death is not an event in life; we do not experience death. – ***Ludwig Wittgenstein***

Gift

Gift is a symbol of affection. When we express our love through the medium of some concrete object, the tender and loving feelings hidden behind it gain importance both for the giver and the receiver of the gift. It is a disgrace if instead of the feelings you value the material worth of the object of gift. A gift is something lovingly given to a person at a particular occasion. So always keep the occasion and the person in mind. When you are giving a gift never let the desire to display prevail on you.

A gift differs from an offering in that it is inspired by affection whereas an offering is actuated more by a feeling of respect and honour for the person and a sense of dedication. What we give our friend on his birthday is a gift whereas what we present at the feet of the Lord in the temple or a teacher is an offering.

The way a gift is presented represents more the character of the giver than that of the receiver. The affectionate feelings of the giver add to the value of the gift.

In our present day society we notice a growing sense of emulation in exchanging gifts. It is a new type of social deformity. Now there is a practice of presenting expensive bouquets as gift and bouquets worth thousands of rupees are presented in a single party. But unfortunately the next morning all the flowers wither, wilt and die. Let us be a little more practical in the matter of gifts. No doubt an exchange of gifts makes our social relations harmonious, but it will be better if our gifts are something useful than just a piece of decoration.

Expensive bouquets may be replaced by books full of noble and inspiring ideas expressed artistically. Books are the best friend of man; they provide him guidance when he is young and solace when he grows old. A good and great book not only bedecks a table or a shelf but changes the direction of one's life. It is a lasting gift and passing through several hands may set new ideas in motion.

If you like, you can give a beautiful, artistic and inspiring painting in place of a book. It will hang all the time in a drawing room and awaken love for art in the heart of all those who happen to cast a glance at it. Thus your painting will instil artistic temperament in a number of viewers.

Add a smiling rose with a book or a painting; it will make your gift fragrant. An exchange of such beautiful and fragrant gifts will portray your good taste, good manners and sensitivity. So present books and works of art and make the gift culture thoughtful and rational. Then your gift will disseminate the sweet smell of dedication, affection and good will.

What Others Say

1. He doubles his gift who gives in time.

2. A small gift is better than a great promise.
   – ***German Proverb***

3. God loveth a cheerful giver. – ***Anon***

4. Giving requires good sense. – ***Ovid***

5. A kind thought has more value than a material gift, because it cannot be bought. – ***N. Sri Ram***

6. Not only is it more blessed to give than to receive it is also delectable. The manner of giving shows the character of the giver, more than the gift itself. – ***Lavater***

7. A fool judges people by the presents they give him.
   – ***Chinese Saying***

8. The manner in which it is given is worth more than the gift. – ***Pierre Corneille***

9. We love those people who give with humility, or who accept with ease. – ***Freya Stark***

10. No person was ever honoured for what he received. Honour has been the reward for what he gave.
    – ***Calvin Coolidge***

Conduct

Conduct means the routine we adopt to manage our life; it reflects our thoughts and manners. The actions, of a person who has noble thoughts are auspicious, but if his thoughts are pernicious his conduct can never be right. Thoughts provide a theoretical mould for conduct. Compassion for ourselves or for others affects our conduct which is an index of our character and personality. Conduct may be silent but it makes a profound impact. Both we and our society evaluate us by our conduct. We should never stoop to take advantage of the goodness of others. Good conduct elevates a person whereas bad conduct puts him on the path of decline; it degrades him in his own eyes, hence good conduct in called life and bad conduct death. Good conduct makes us judicious and discerning which is preferable to be learned. We have always affirmed that the one who behaves wisely has realized God. The life of a discreet person is always peaceful and buoyant. Shruti says: Blessed are those that like the sea are serious and patient by nature; they never brag about their marvellous achievements; their conduct is rational and wakeful. Those who fail to discern between good and bad conduct are groping in the dark. One who behaves outrageously is most ill-starred because no one comes to his help when he falls on evil days. Indian tradition has it that those who sympathise with the miserable have no chance to feel distressed themselves and those who are jubilant over others' happiness have not to exert for their own happiness. They are liberal and join hearts. They believe in building bridges in the family or society instead of raising barriers and dividers.

The basic principle of good conduct is: Don't earn your living in a sinful way, and indulge not in things that augment your anxiety. Don't spend so much that you must incur debt and don't eat excessively that you fall ill. The one who has such a positive outlook on life speaks, moves, eats, drinks and thinks not for himself alone but for the good of all. He does everything for their welfare and his life is free from deceit and dissembling. The conduct of one who considers simplicity a great virtue of life and believes in meeting the expectations of others as his own hopes is exemplary. But the life of a dissembler lacks equilibrium to regain which he must do what he says and say what he does. The greatest weakness of man today is that he boasts of high ideals but does not live up to them himself. Unless we get rid of these common paradoxes we cannot ascertain faith in life. Those who talk of being faithful have faith in wealth and fame, children and family. We must dedicate ourselves to high human values and when our life shapes accordingly, our birth and life on this earth will be well rewarded.

What Others Say

1. Let us endeavour so to live that when we come to die even the undertaker will he sorry. – ***Mark Twain***
2. No one knows about your integrity, your sincerity, your talent or your goodness unless you give out samples in action. – ***W J. H. Boetcker***
3. The sum of behaviour is to retain man's own dignity without intruding upon the liberty of others. – ***Francis Bacon***
4. When you change your behaviour, you change your performance and you change your life. – ***Anonymous.***
5. Conduct is three-fourth of our life and its largest concern. – ***Mathew Arnold***
6. The integrity of men is to be measured by their conduct, not by their profession. – ***Anonymous***

7. The force that rules the world is conduct, whether it be moral or immoral. – ***Nicholas Murray***

8. The reputation of a thousand years may be determined by the conduct of one hour. – ***Japanese Proverb***

9. Ask any decent person what he thinks matters most in human conduct : five to one his answer will be 'kindness'. – ***Kenneth Clark***

10. Absolute morality is the regulation of conduct in such a way that pain shall not be inflicted. – ***Herbert Spencer***

Goal

A man has a certain goal when he attempts to do a thing, for he cannot do anything if he has no aim. If he does any thing aimlessly it ends in fiasco. Our faith in achieving our object is called our goal. Life is a journey and every journey has a destination. Those who travel aimlessly are like the galley slave and reach nowhere in spite of all their labour. The phrase much ado about nothing perfectly applies to them. Our journey is fulfilled only when we have some end in view, otherwise it is nothing more than a circumambulation.

Before embarking on an undertaking one thinks why he wants to attempt it. The answer to this 'why' serves as the goal. What is the goal of life? If we start exploring the answer to this question we shall reach the conclusion that it is spending a successful, noble and happy life. From the spiritual point of view the highest aim of life is the realization of God and a state of blessedness.

There is no life without an aim. Always keep your aim before your eyes, dream of it and live for it. When you find the right means of realizing it, move forward. If you wander aimlessly making vain efforts here and there you will not achieve anything. Fix a target and work for it and you will surely be rewarded with success. So set a goal of your life and assiduously work for it, for you cannot hope to realize it unless you make efforts.

Some people are torn with anxiety about their aim. They don't think in the right direction and their inner-self roams around in a blind alley. In fact, instead of worrying about your goal think rationally and hopefully, move towards it and you will achieve what you have planned..

To ensure our success we must be fully dedicated to our goal, for in its absence we cannot achieve anything. The dedication must be as intense as the goal is high. If we wish that the Ganga should descend from the heaven we should be willing to make herculean efforts like Bhagirath.

Dedication must also be reinforced by a firm resolution because the power of resolution can overcome any obstacle any opposition on the way of realizing our goal. Dedication and resolution are the two wheels of the chariot moving towards our goal. When they are in perfect harmony, the chariot will run smoothly on the path of progress.

Like Arjuna we should focus on the bull's eye and make our thought, conduct and consciousness all converge in the right direction to overcome every challenge. Man wants to achieve success but these days he is running in the direction opposite the door of success. If we run against our goal, we may go round and round the whole world but shall never reach our destination. If we turn to the right direction we shall stand face to face with our goal. In the present circumstances of life, man needs guidance, for in the absence of guidance he cannot change the circumstances. Hit at the right direction and the goal will greet you with open arms.

What Others Say

1. If you don't aim at something, you will never hit anything. *– El. H. Christians*

2. A man must have his dreams – memory dreams of the past and eager dreams of the future. I never want to stop reaching for new goals. *– Maurice Chevalier*

3. Goals are dreams with deadlines. *– Diana Scharf Hunt*

4. The trouble with not having a goal is that you can spend your life running up and down the field and never scoring. *– Bill Copeland*

5. In the long run men hit only what they aim at. *– Henry David Thoreau*

6. Goals determine what you are going to be. *– Julius Erving*

7. The trouble with our age is that it is all signposts and no destination.

8. When you aim for perfection, you discover it's a moving target. *– George Fisher*

9. Whoever wants to reach a distant goal must take many small steps. *– Helmut Schmidt*

10. One who thinks in terms of silver, cannot act in terms of gold. *– Henry G. Weaver*

11. If we make it our first goal to please God, it solves many problems at once. *– Philip E. Howard*

12. Before you score, you must have a goal. *– Proverb*

Music

Music is the language of soul. Listening to soft lilting music soothes and calms mind, it builds a bridge between the two worlds – temporal and transcendental. When we listen to music a spring of joy seems to rise in our heart, soul and consciousness. All our anxiety and mental steadiness pauses for a moment. Music is such a divine blessing. It is an art.

Music is both vocal and instrumental. It soothes the mind, cures disease and purifies feelings. When the love for music crosses its zenith, it generates divine feelings in mind.

In the voice of music speaks spirituality, love both earthly and divine hums to express itself. All religions use music as accompaniment of worshipping God. Music creates a comforting atmosphere that overwhelms the heart, heightens devotion and prevails on mind to assimilate God. Through music, the devotees pour out their adoration for God, the lovers their distress. Music enchants not only human beings but also birds and beasts.

A prevalent belief has it that the thrilling resonance produced by a Veena so captivates the deer that the hunters could easily shoot them. A deer loves the soothing music more than his life. Melodious music flowing from the snake charmer's pipe makes the large venomous snakes raise and sway their head. Music is praised as the fifth Veda. Infact, all the four Vedas are highly metrical compositions. Each verse in the Koran is so mellifluous that it appears overflowing with joy. There is a continuous stream of music flowing from the Vedic prayers to the present day hymns. It seems that music came into existence in the very inception of civilization. It permeates every element in nature. Clouds begin to pour when the Raga Malhar is played and the Deepak Raga lights the lamps. Strange is the world of music. The hobby is very charming. When you are fully steeped in music your whole existence seems to become musical.

A man must have an aptitude for one of these accomplishments – literature, music and fine art. He must absorb himself wholeheartedly in any one of them. The Hitopadesha rightly says that a man indifferent to these is verily a beast without a tail and horns. What can we say about those who do not take to music even after this bitter remark!

What Others Say

1. The other arts persuade up, but music takes us by surprise. *– Eduard Hanslick*
2. Without music, life is a journey through a desert. *– Pat Conroy*
3. Music washes away from the soul the dust of everyday life. *– Berthold Auerbach*
4. Where words fail, music speaks. *– Hans Christian Andersen*
5. It is only by introducing the young to great literature, drama and music that we open to them the possibilities that lie within the human spirit – enable them to see visions and dream dreams. *– Eric Anderson*
6. Where there's music, there can be no evil. *– Cervantes*
7. What passion cannot music raise and quell? *– John Dryden*
8. Music hath charms to soothe the savage breast. *– William Congreve*

9. In sweet music is such art,
Killing care and grief of heart. – ***Anonymous***

10. There is no feeling, except the extremes of fear and grief that does not find relief in music. – ***George Eliot***

11. Music is the speech of angels. – ***Thomas Carlyle***

12. Music is the language of the spirit, it opens the secret of life bringing peace, abolishing strife. – ***Kahlil Gibran***

Success

Everyone knows the value of labour in life. Only the tree of hard work bears the fruit of success. Labour is the essence of man's vigour, success, its adornment. A simple and plain definition of success is that it is the fulfilment of our resolutions. In life we are always busy doing something, for we cherish a goal. We study, appear at the examination and pass it. Clearing the examination expresses our success. The achievement of our goal in any field of life is called success.

For achieving success both the means and the end should be pure. Tenacity, self-confidence and resoluteness prepare the ground for success. Success depends on our resolution, so we should remember God before starting anything. If we have faith in God we will never fail. Nothing is impossible for a man of resolution willing to act on it. We can estimate our success from the faith others repose in us. We need more effort to maintain our success than to achieve it.

Shruti also says: It is more difficult to maintain success than to attain it. It is surprising that most of the people love success but envy those that are successful. If we respect them we can learn the secret of success. If we adopt in our life the qualities that they possess, we shall also achieve it. We can succeed if we are willing to learn from our failures. A really successful person is one who plays to win, learns from others' mistakes, returns more than what he receives, acts prudently, measures his strength before taking a decision, never compromises with honesty and regards success a blessing from God.

We must make sustained efforts to achieve success. Small efforts open the gate of great success. There is no shortcut to success and the success we get by shortcut does not last long. To attain success, we must work very hard, have firm determination and be ready to sacrifice even our life to gain our end. Those that are determined to succeed even at the cost of their life and are willing to work hard are sure to succeed. The winners do not do anything new but do it in a new way.

The quality most essential for success is mental preparedness. We must continue working without vacillating for vacillation and success never go hand in hand. Failure very often creates distraction and obstruction on the path of success. Remember, if one wants to pick roses one is very likely to be pierced and injured by thorns, but a man of determination never gives in. Success never greets one who succumbs to obstruction and opposition.

As the dawn emerges from the womb of might, success emerges from the womb of failure. The sun sets and then rises again the next day. The flowers whither in the evening but again blossom next morning, similarly a man should prepare to welcome success after failure. Those that make effort never lose, for them every failure is a positive step in the direction of success.

What others say

1. Success is never final and failure never total. It's courage that counts.
2. Success covers a multitude of blunders.
   – ***Bernard Shaw***
3. Failure is the condiment that gives success its flavour.
   – ***Truman Capote***
4. True success is overcoming the fear of being unsuccessful. – ***Paul Sweeney***
5. Success is getting what you want. – ***H. Jackson Brown***

6. Always bear in mind that your own resolution to succeed is more important than anyone thing.
   – Abraham Lincoln
7. Striving for success without hard work is like trying to harvest where you haven't planted. ***– David Bly***
8. There are no secrets to success. It is the result of preparation, hard work, learning from failure.
   – Gen. Colin L. Powell
9. To become an able and successful man in any profession, three things are necessary nature, study and practice. ***– Walt Mason***
10. Success often comes to those who dare and act, it seldom goes to the timid who are ever afraid of consequences. ***– Jawaharlal Nehru***
11. The secret of success in life is for a man to be ready for his opportunity when it comes. ***– Benjamin Disralli***
12. Success is a ladder which cannot be climbed with your hands in your pockets.